Edward Strachey

Talk at a Country House

Fact and fiction

Edward Strachey

Talk at a Country House
Fact and fiction

ISBN/EAN: 9783337231699

Printed in Europe, USA, Canada, Australia, Japan

Cover: Foto ©Thomas Meinert / pixelio.de

More available books at **www.hansebooks.com**

TALK AT A COUNTRY HOUSE

THIS BOOK

IS INSCRIBED

TO MY CHILDREN

WHOSE LOVE AND CARE HAVE MADE FOR ME

A HAPPY OLD AGE

AND ESPECIALLY TO

MY DAUGHTER FRANCES

WHOSE CONSTANT AND UNTIRING SERVICES

HAVE MORE THAN SUPPLIED THE PLACE

OF FAILING EYESIGHT

AND SO TURNED LOSS TO GAIN.

CONTENTS

I.

THE SQUIRE AND HIS OLD MANOR PLACE.

The Squire and his old House. — Arrival. — Talk about
Building Bess. — Berowne's Oak. — Love's Labour 's
Lost. — Idea or Motive of the Play 1

II.

PERSIAN POETRY.

The Giant's Wall. — The Rose Garden. — Persian Poetry.
— Muhammedan and Christian Mystics. — The Atábaks. — The Use and Disuse of Persian in India . . 14

III.

THE OLD HALL AND THE PORTRAITS.

The Old Hall. — The Children dancing. — The Portraits.
— John Locke and John Strachey, Clive, Watson, Kirkpatrick. — Burke and Sir William Jones. — The Nego-
tiation with the United States 41

IV.

A GENERAL ELECTION : RIGHT AND WRONG IN POLITICS.

A General Election. — The Candidature. — The Polling
Day. — Before and after the Ballot Act. — Counting

the Votes. — The Winner and his Welcome Home. —
The Morality of the Ballot 66

V.

LOVE AND MARRIAGE.

A Country Wedding. — The Village Church. — The Village Home. — Wedding Breakfasts. — Love and Marriage. — Death and Life 94

VI.

BOOKS: TENNYSON AND MAURICE.

Books. — The Bible and Shakespeare. — Paradise Lost
and the Pilgrim's Progress. — The Riddle of the
Sphinx. — Crossing the Bar. — The Poet and the
Prophet. — The Crimean War. — The King's College
Story 121

VII.

RIDING DOWN TO CAMELOT.

The Camelot and Arthur of History. — Of Local Tradition and Legend. — Of Romance. — Of Modern
Poetry. — Chivalry. — Sir Thomas Malory. — Idylls
of the King 150

VIII.

THE ARROWHEADED INSCRIPTIONS.

Decipherment. — Criticism and Divination. — Ideographic
and Alphabetical Writing. — Assyrian Annals. — Light
thrown on Jewish History. — German Criticism. —
How estimated by Grote 179

IX.

TAKING LEAVE.

Taking Leave. — Émile Souvestre. — Old Age. — Memory. — Pope and Parnell. — Edward Lear. — A Retrospect 209

APPENDIX.

Introduction to the Būstān or Garden of Sa'di, translated from the Persian 237

TALK AT A COUNTRY HOUSE

I.

THE SQUIRE AND HIS OLD MANOR PLACE.

> And one, an English home, — gray twilight pour'd
> On dewy pastures, dewy trees,
> Softer than sleep, — all things in order stored,
> A haunt of ancient Peace.
>
> PALACE OF ART.

WHILE traveling abroad some years ago I had made the acquaintance of an old Somersetshire country gentleman : we had become

> "A pair of friends, though I was young,
> And Matthew seventy-two,"

and now, on my coming back to England, he had invited me to pay him a visit.

The Squire, as his family and his neighbors called him, was past work, as he used to say, but not past the enjoyments of an old age spent in the home which he shared with his children and grandchildren. And as he loved his bit of Chaucer, he would apply to himself the description of the Clerk, —

> "And gladly would he learn and gladly teach."

He liked to talk of the old house which I was
now about to see. And I think that my friend's
character as I knew him had been a good deal
formed by the influences of the house in which
he was born and looked to die. Though he
mourned the destruction of some very old features of the house, and the things in it, some
of which had still existed in his own childhood, yet he had made like changes when he
himself came into possession ; and he used to
say that he had the authority of Carlyle and
Maurice for so doing — the former advising
him ever to join the new with the old, and the
latter not to scruple to make the house he
was to live in fitting in all respects for his
own generation. He loved books of all kinds,
but poetry and history most of all : and I fancied when I came to know him in his old hall
and parlor, as well as under his old trees,
that these things had both limited and deep-
ened his reading. He used to say that his
motto was " Multum non multa," which he
translated " Not many things, but much of two
or three."

He loved what have been called the by-
ways of history. " Why," he would say, " go
along the dusty high road, when you may get
to the same place by the path across the fields,
and have shrubs and flowers, and the songs of
the birds, all along, instead of the dust." And

when I reminded him of what came to Christian and Hopeful in his favorite " Pilgrim's Progress," when they preferred the walk through the fields, he only answered with a smile : —

"John P.
Robinson, he
Sez they did n't know everythin' down in Judee."

From the railway station I drove along the road by which Leland had ridden four hundred and fifty years before, when he was on the like errand to my own, that of visiting the old Manor Place of Southetoune. Now, as then, the road was " meatly well woddyd."

Evening was coming on when I drove through the lodge gates. The air was resonant with the cawing of the rooks as they filled the sky with the circles in which they wheeled to and fro, disappearing in the distance, to appear again, and so gradually reach their roosting-trees. In spite of their blackness where they did not catch and reflect back the rays of the setting sun, I might call them a coruscation of rooks, so much did they remind me of the Roman *Girandola*, when the sky was filled with its countless flights of rockets. I saw before me, and on my right hand, two giant arbors — " aisles," Tennyson would have called them — of lime-trees, feathering to the ground, and seeming to reach the very sky ; while between

them opened out an avenue of immemorial
elms. On my left I saw, as Leland had seen
them before me, the old battlemented wall and
the square tower with its corner turret rising
behind and above the wall, and a succession
of gables on either side ; and among them I
saw one marked by a cross which I knew must
be that of the chapel which my old friend had
told me of, as the work of Building Bess of
Hardwicke, afterwards Countess of Shrews-
bury. Like the Roman Coliseum before it was
scraped by the modern reformers, the old battlemented wall had a flora of its own : ferns,
crimson valerian, snapdragons, and briar roses,
and along with these I saw an ash and a yew
growing on the battlements, where they had
been sown no doubt by the rooks. And as I
passed through an archway in the wall, the
whole house came in view. It was not a castle,
nor a palace, but it might be called a real
though small record of what men had been
doing there from the time of Domesday Book
to our own.

The Squire welcomed me with his usual
heartiness, introducing me to the ladies of the
family, and then adding : " But you know Foster
already : you have often met him at Headlong
Hall. I am glad he has not brought Mr. Escot
with him." The Squire was fond of quoting
Peacock's derivation of the name of Foster in

" Headlong Hall," as that of " one who watches over and guards the light," telling us that it suited my habit of asking questions.

Next morning we had breakfast in a parlor the oak paneling and carved mantelpiece of which, the Squire said, were among the embellishments of the old manor place made by Building Bess of Hardwicke, to one of whose four husbands the house belonged. After breakfast we walked together down the steps of the terraces, and through the avenue of huge lime-trees and oaks, which my host told me were all planted by the same great lady. My thoughts wandered from that imperious dame to her still more imperious mistress, Queen Elizabeth, and from Queen Elizabeth to Shakespeare, and so to the Forest of Arden and to the park of the king of Navarre. It was in the leafy month of June. The air was fragrant with honeysuckle and sweetbrier growing along the banks of a brook hidden from sight, but telling of itself by the pleasant noise of a little waterfall into which it was breaking ; and the musical hum of unseen insects was all around, through which was now and then heard the cooing of a wood pigeon hidden somewhere in the trees. We stopped under a great oak, and sat down in the shade, on a mossy seat formed by the roots of the tree.

"What are you thinking of?" said the Squire, who had been silent since he had finished pointing out the works of the lady I have named.

I answered that I was thinking this was the oak in the branches of which Berowne lay hid while he listened to the talk of the king and his other lords.

"I am glad to hear you call him, as Shakespeare himself did, ' Berowne.' I respect as well as like the Cambridge editors, but I cannot conceive why they should substitute the spelling of the Second Folio, which has no authority, for that of the Quarto and the First Folio."

My old friend seemed inclined to be warm on this point, so I turned the subject by saying, " I know you do not make much account of internal evidence, but do you not think there is something in the case of ' Love's Labour 's Lost ' to show that it was one of the earliest of Shakespeare's plays ? "

The Squire. I can seldom find that the so-called internal evidence as to the date of any book is more than critical, that is more or less ingenious, conjecture. Where are you to stop if, after finding all the buoyancy and brightness of youth in this play, you go on (like Hallam, if I remember rightly) to discover a disappointed, it may be melancholy, and even

a misanthropical Shakespeare in " Hamlet "
and " Timon," drawn from the experiences of
manhood and old age ?

Foster. I confess that internal evidence is
for the most part like a circle in the water, —

> " Which never ceaseth to enlarge itself,
>   Till, by broad spreading, it disperse to nought."

Yet does not the circle start from a real stone
thrown in ?

The Squire. Or from some bubble rising
from we know not where ? Yet I am inclined
to yield to you here, and to make an exception
in favor of the indications that this was one of
the earliest, if not the earliest, of Shakespeare's
plays. Ferdinand and Miranda, Romeo and
Juliet, are even more perfect representatives
of the youth and maiden than are Berowne and
Rosaline ; yet while these last require only that
the poet's pen should be dipped in ink " temper'd by Love's sighs," it may have been that
the others could not have been depicted but
by an eye

> " That hath kept watch o'er man's mortality."

Besides, " I too once lived in Arcady," and I
should like to hear what you have still to say
of the idea, or, as I suppose people would now
call it, the motive, of " Love's Labour 's Lost,"
and what it may possibly tell us of the poet
himself, and so of its probable date.

Foster. I can hardly pretend to add anything to what Coleridge has already said on the subject.

The Squire. There is, indeed, not much more to be said when Coleridge has spoken, and his words have come down to us ; yet — forgive the impertinence — a dwarf on a giant's shoulders may see farther than the giant himself.

Foster. Artists say that a portrait, while it must be true to nature and a likeness of the individual whom it represents, must, if it be a true work of art, show the idea, or motive, either of calm repose or of the animation of the moment in which one characteristic expression is passing into another. And the motive of this play may, I think, be said to be youth at the moment of passing into manhood and womanhood. Boys and girls become dignified men and women before our eyes ; and it is love which makes the magic change, — a change which Berowne describes in words so burning yet so pure and chaste, so passionate yet spiritual, that I, at least, can never read or repeat them too often : —

> " Other slow arts entirely keep the brain ;
> And therefore, finding barren practisers,
> Scarce show a harvest of their heavy toil :
> But love, first learned in a lady's eyes,
> Lives not alone immured in the brain ;
> But, with the motion of all elements,

Courses as swift as thought in every power,
And gives to every power a double power,
Above their functions and their offices.
It adds a precious seeing to the eye ;
A lover's eyes will gaze an eagle blind ;
A lover's ear will hear the lowest sound,
When the suspicious head of theft is stopp'd :
Love's feeling is more soft and sensible
Than are the tender horns of cockled snails ;
Love's tongue proves dainty Bacchus gross in taste :
For valour, is not Love a Hercules,
Still climbing trees in the Hesperides ?
Subtle as Sphinx ; as sweet and musical
As bright Apollo's lute, strung with his hair :
And when Love speaks, the voice' of all the gods
Make heaven drowsy with the harmony.
Never durst poet touch a pen to write
Until his ink were temper'd with Love's sighs ;
O, then his lines would ravish savage ears
And plant in tyrants mild humility.
From women's eyes this doctrine I derive :
They sparkle still the right Promethean fire ;
They are the books, the arts, the academes,
That show, contain and nourish all the world :
Else none at all in aught proves excellent."

The Squire. They are indeed perfect ; and
we may well say with Berowne that when such
" Love speaks, the voice' of all the gods make
heaven drowsy with the harmony." Does not
Coleridge say that this speech is that of the
very god of love himself ? But go on.

Foster. The ladies in the play, as in nature,
are at first inclined to make fun of the serious
ardor of their admirers, till the whole scene
becomes a tilting-match or tournament of wits,

in which — again with truth to nature — the
ladies get the better, and the men confess
themselves "beaten with pure scoff." But Love
is becoming lord of all with the ladies, too.
Another transition is marked when the princess
exclaims, "We are wise girls to mock our lovers
so!" Then come the tidings of the death of
her father, the king of France. In a moment
the electric spark crystallizes that life of fun
and joyousness. The generous and noble-
minded youths and maidens become, as I have
said, dignified men and women, and turn to
the duties of real life, though agreeing that the
new is still to be linked with the old. If the
poet had told us the real ending, he would
have called the play "Love's Labour 's Won,"
and so anticipated the answer to a still vexed
question of Dr. Dryasdust.

The Squire. Well done! I wish every one
knew, and then he would prize this play as
you do. But how does all this prove the early
date of the play?

Foster. You yourself said just now that you
were inclined to recognize a distinction between the creations of Ferdinand and Miranda,
and Romeo and Juliet, and those of Berowne
and Rosaline. I think this is so, and that we
must not look in this play for the expression
of that mature genius which we find in the later
works. But of the genius itself, not yet ma-

ture, we have abundant tokens; and here is, in truth, one especial charm and interest of this play. How pleasant it is to look at the portraits of Milton, the child, the youth, and the man, and to trace the lineaments of moral and intellectual as well as physical beauty in their successive developments, — the child surviving in the man, and the man fulfilling the promise of the child! And though no such portraiture of Shakespeare's face in youth exists for us, we have the portrait of his mind in its successive stages of growth, if we follow Ben Jonson's advice and

> " looke
> Not on his picture, but his Booke;"

and again : —

> " Look, how the father's face
> Lives in his issue; even so the race
> Of Shakespeare's mind and manners brightly shines
> In his well turnèd and true filèd lines."

The Squire. You remember that Ben Jonson said something on the other side, — that he wished Shakespeare had blotted a thousand lines.

Foster. Yes, but the reconciliation is obvious as we read; for we know Shakespeare does write with an accuracy as well as profoundness of thought which must have been the fruit of the highest intellectual training and culture; with an ease and a fluency of utterance which sometimes verges on carelessness and negligence of language, and shows especially when the poet is under the influence of his love of fun. But his play of "Love's Labour's Lost" is remarkable for its careful accuracy of thought and word even in its fun, and indicates how much Shakespeare must, in the days of his earliest compositions, have studied the logical use of language, even when he is employing it to express the most fanciful conceits or the most soaring imaginations. The play is full of instances of this careful composition, with its regular balance of thoughts, words, and rhymes in the successive lines. This use of language is perfect in its kind; yet how different it is from that of "The Tempest," "Othello," or "Hamlet"! Surely, the difference between the youthful and the mature genius is plain enough.

The Squire. Yes, and you have made a good defense — or explanation shall I call it? — of Coleridge's saying that this play is like a portrait of the poet taken in his boyhood. And let me confess to you that when I was young I myself wrote an argument in the same sense, endeavoring to show, by an analysis of Berowne's speech against learning, how exactly it must have represented Shakespeare's own experiences and conclusions as to the relations between the study of books and the knowledge of life, when he first came up to London with his small Latin and less Greek.[1]

Then we got up, and walked to the wooden bridge which crossed the brook just above the waterfall ; and I saw the small red and blue dragonflies and one great brown one — so formidable looking, though so harmless — darting to and fro over the water ; and a kingfisher shot, flashing in the sunlight, from a hawthorn bush upon the bank.

[1] *Fraser's Magazine*, January, 1858, p. 41.

II.

PERSIAN POETRY.

The roses of this garden will not fade.

SA'DI.

THE Squire loved his limes, elms, and oaks, but he loved his roses, too. They festooned the transoms of the old mullioned windows of the parlor, and might be gathered from the casement of my lady's chamber; and they stood in array under the shelter of what still remained of the great battlemented wall, which had once protected the house and tower against arrows and bolts as it still did from the north winds. The Squire told me tradition related that this wall was built by the Norman giant, St. Loe, who lived in the tower. This tradition was authenticated by the fact that a neighboring giant, Hakewell, whose quoit still remains in witness, on passing by asked what he was building this wall for; and when he was answered, "To keep out such fellows as you," Hakewell at once stepped over it; and the effigies of both giants, one in oak and the other in stone, may still be seen in the parish church. Leland, indeed, writing in Henry VIII.'s time, says only, "Here hath Sir John St. Loe an old manor place," and adds that the monument of his grandfather is in the church. Modern archæologists, moreover, declare that the quoit is only one of the huge Druidical stones of which more than one circle remains hard by. But the wall itself, as I have said, stands there to testify, and to shelter the Squire's roses.

He was gathering a nosegay of these when I joined him. As he stood by a great bush of the kind called "maiden blush," he gently shook from a flower one of those bright green rose-chafers which live on that rose, repeating, as it flew off, "A mailed angel on a battle day." I said, "Why do you drive away the pretty creature?" "Because I might have 'maiden shriek' for 'maiden blush,'" he answered, "if I were to offer a young lady a green beetle with my roses." He walked toward a carriage, which I had not seen before, in which were a mother and daughter, who had been among the visitors, and were now taking leave. I could not hear what he said, as he gave a nosegay to each lady with his wonted old-fashioned gallantry; but I might guess that it was "Sweets to the sweet." Then, as the carriage rolled through the gateway in the old wall, he turned toward the house, repeating some words which, from the half-chanting sound, I knew to be something from the

Persian, which he was always fond of quoting to himself. Then we talked on.

Foster. I like to hear the musical and melodious sound of Persian, though I do not understand the meaning. But were you taking leave of the ladies in Persian?

The Squire. Only a poet can translate poetry; but come into the Great Parlor, and I will try to find you a better translation than my own would be of what I said.

Foster. Why do you and your children call it the " Great Parlor," while other people call it the "library"?

The Squire. It is the old name; perhaps given it by Bess of Hardwicke herself, when she built it, and the chapel over it, because she was not content with the "little parlor," which was enough for the forefathers of her husband, St. Loe. Bookshelves have now taken the place of her oak paneling; but I fancy her still sitting in one of the deep window-seats, and looking up at her great coat of arms over the mantelpiece, impaled with that of her husband, and with more quarterings than I can remember the names of. Now for the books.

Foster. But you have not yet told me the name of the book you were quoting, nor its author.

The Squire. It is the "Gūlistān," or Rose Garden, of Sa'di. Many who have a far better

right than I to speak on the subject say that it is
the greatest work of the greatest of the Persian
poets. It has been translated into Latin, English, German, French, and perhaps other languages. There are at least four English translations, which you will find on that shelf.

Foster. A great witness to the worth of the
original. How every man who has drunk deeply
of Homer, Horace, or Dante tries to translate
his favorite author, in order that others may
share with him the enjoyment which, while it
remains unshared, seems scarcely his own !

The Squire. Every one tries, and every one
fails. The thought, the habit of mind, is as
different in one country and one age from that
of another as is the language ; and what genius
is sufficient to reproduce the original thought
in a wholly new form, and to express it in new
words as exactly fitted to the thought as are
those of the first writer ! The English Bible —
not the Revised Version — is almost an exception ; but then Hebrew thought has, through
long ages, become the thought of Christendom,
and is in a measure as English as English itself.
Even so, it is wonderful that such a translation
into such English should have been possible.

Foster. You were to show me a translation
of the passage which you were quoting from
Sa'di : which am I to take ?

The Squire. That of Eastwick is probably the

most scholarly, and he represents the original
alternations of prose and verse in a way which
is often happy; but I sometimes rather fancy
the quaintness of Dumoulin. There it is. But
if the subject interests you enough, you should
read the whole of Sa'di's Introduction, or preface, which in this, as in his " Būstān," is to
European taste, at least, the finest part of either
book. But for the " Būstān " I must refer you
to a translation of my own.[1] And then, after all
our disparagement of translations, if only you
will, with Tennyson, spread the silken sail of
infancy and call back your old visions of the
Arabian Nights. I think you will be repaid for
your trouble, though you do not find all that
the readers of the original talk of.

Foster. Meanwhile, Squire, will you give me
an outline of the country you advise me to
enter on ?

The Squire. The " Būstān," or Garden, and
the " Gūlistān," or Rose Garden, have the same
idea or motive, though there is great variety in
the treatment. The Introduction to each opens
with the praises of God, taking as it were for
text the words with which the devout Mussul-
man always begins to speak or write, " In the
Name of God, the Merciful, the Compassion-
ate." The outburst of beauty which clothes the
earth in the season of spring, the gift of life and

1 See Appendix.

articulate speech to man, the divine government of the world, the blessings of which are shared by the good and bad alike, — all these declare the wisdom, goodness, and greatness of the Creator, and call for thankfulness from man. Sa'di's piety, and the political genius which that piety inspires and informs, are very striking. He writes in a manner which reminds one of the spirit of Isaiah or of Milton.

Explain it or leave it unexplained as you may, the fact cannot be denied of the contrast — the difference in kind between the religions of Greece and Rome and the faith of Islam, and the likeness in kind between the latter and the Christian faith. And this was evidently the genuine and practical faith of Sa'di; he was eminently a religious man, believing in an actual relation between God and man. And the wreck and anarchy of nations which the Tartar devastation had caused around him, contrasted with the beneficent reign of such rulers as his own, directed all his thoughts and hopes to the belief in a constitutional government of the world, old and settled on the foundations of eternal law and justice and mercy, under a righteous king. The "Gūlistān" opens with a description of springtime: the "Būstān" by setting forth the attributes of the Creator. From this praise of the Creator Sa'di goes on to speak of the Prophet; and then of the righteous rule of the

Atābak, or sovereign, Aboo-Bakr, in whose reign he was writing. In a day when the prosperity and happiness of a whole people were always dependent on the character of a ruler, Sa'di is never weary of insisting on the duties of kings, justice, mercy, beneficence, and the maintenance of all these by a strong hand; and while the former annals of Persia treat of many such kings, he declares that none of them was more worthy than Aboo-Bakr. Then, with the proud humility of a great man conscious of his genius, he says that lowly as he is in the presence of his king, yet it is his verses — the pearls of poetry which he is stringing — which shall keep that king's memory alive in the coming ages.

Foster. But, Squire, you have not told me what you said after speeding the ladies on their way.

The Squire. You find me " as tedious as a king," though you have not Dogberry's appreciation of that virtue. But I was just coming to the point. Sa'di goes on, in the Introduction to each book, to give his reasons for writing it, in the form of an apologue. In the " Gūlistān," he tells, in a charming idyl, how, when he had become a dervish, and was sitting in the corner of retirement and meditation, he was prevailed on, by the entreaties of an old friend, to spend the evening outside the city, in a garden spark-

ling and fragrant with flowers and cool with
fountains. In the morning, when the desire
to depart had overcome the wish to stay, Sa'di's
friend gathered a nosegay of roses, hyacinths,
and sweet basil for him to take, but threw them
down when the poet, reminding him that such
flowers must soon fade and die, promised to
write him a book which should live. And on
the same day he began the "Gūlistān."

Foster. Then the ladies should have thrown
away your roses while you made your speech
in Persian. But what is the corresponding
apologue?

The Squire. In the "Būstān," Sa'di describes
himself as spending his days with men of every
kind, in every corner of the world, and gathering some treasure from every store, and some
ears of corn from every harvest. But he found
no people like those of Shiraz, his native city.
He could not leave such a people empty-
handed, and he resolved to write a book in
their honor and memory; to build a palace of
art and education, of which the ten gates, or
chapters, should be Justice and Judgment;
Beneficence, by which man may show the likeness of God; Love, not earthly, but divine;
Humility; Resignation; Contentment; Education; Thankfulness; Repentance and Righteousness; and lastly, Prayer.

Foster. Are not the Atábaks, as you call

them, the Atabegs, as the name used to be
written before the invention of the scientific
method of spelling Oriental words by help of a
key? If I remember rightly, it is a Turkish
word, meaning " Protector of the Prince," and
was an official title.

The Squire. Yes ; and on the break-up of the
Seljuk dynasty, in the twelfth century of our
era, like mayors of the palace and other such
ministers in old times and places, they sup-
planted their sovereigns, and founded dynasties
of their own. There were four such dynasties
in Persia, of which that of Aboo-Bakr was one.
His capital was Shiraz ; and though the Turks
and Tartars destroyed the civilization and culture of the West, they roused to new activity
the letters and science which the Arabs had
carried into Persia, and those adjoining countries in which Persian was the language of
the court and of literature. After allowing for
the flights of Oriental imagination on the one
hand, and for the shortcomings of a translation on the other, even the English reader can
see that Sa'di's thoughts and words of God
and of man, of nature and of civil government,
betoken a high degree of culture and refine-
ment, and the practice of wise, just, and righteous government by the kings ; and those who
know the original agree that for happiness and
beauty of imagery and language it may com-

pare with the poetry of other nations, while in depth of pathos it far surpasses that of Greece or Rome. Persian poetry draws its main spirit from Hebrew and early Christian sources, though through the channel of Muhammedanism; and we may say that it rises above or falls below the classical standards much as these do.

Foster. What else did Sa'di write?

The Squire. The list of his works is long, but his " Diwān," or Collection of Songs of Mystical Piety, has been overshadowed by that of Hafiz; and the works by which he is chiefly known are those of which we have already spoken.

Foster. What is known of Sa'di himself?

The Squire. He mentions in several places incidents in his own life; and these were put together, with the addition of some traditions, by a Persian writer, two hundred years later. He is said to have spent thirty years in study, thirty in traveling in distant lands, and thirty in retirement as a dervish. He was taken prisoner by the crusaders while practicing austerities in the desert, and made to work on the fortifications of Tripoli; and he was redeemed by an old friend, whose daughter he afterwards married. She was a Persian Xanthippe, and when she cast in his teeth that her father had bought him for ten dinars, he replied that he had sold himself again for one hundred, the amount of her dowry. But, so far as I know, the fullest account of Sa'di is to be found in the introduction to Harrington's edition of the works of Sa'di (Sadee, he calls him), published in Calcutta in 1791.

(Here our talk ended, for that morning. But we returned to the subject some days later; and I now give the substance of the conversation which then followed between the Squire and myself.)

Foster. Since our talk the other day about Persian poetry, I have been looking into the books you pointed out to me, and into the translations of Omar Khayyām by Fitzgerald, Whinfield, and McCarthy, and of Hafiz by Reviski, Bicknell, and Clarke.

The Squire. Omar, the skeptic and mathematician, in the century before, and Hafiz, the religious mystic, in the century after, that of Sa'di, the political philosopher and theologian. And, to use a favorite Persian metaphor, all these pearls of poesy are strung on the chronological tables of Malcolm's " History of Persia ; " though he hardly mentions these or any other of the great Persian poets. But have you found any new clues to the philosophy of history, either with or without the help of our Anglo-Persian Dryasdusts ?

Foster. You always laugh at my philosophy of history ; but if philosophy is the search for wisdom, and if reason is ratio, or the relation of things to one another, why should it be unreasonable to seek for the relations of the facts of history?

The Squire. Not at all unreasonable to seek what yet it may be impossible to find. Bacon says that all facts are governed by laws, and that these laws are ideas in the mind of God; but then another authority, not less than Bacon, says, " His ways are past finding out." It is a grand and glorious moment in a young man's life when, after years of toiling up the schoolboy's hill of facts, he reaches a point at which the scene of history as one great whole bursts on his astonished view. I do not forget the delight with which I first read Arnold's account of Vico's comparison of the history of a nation with the life of a man, with its three stages of childhood, manhood, and old age; or again of Comte's three historical periods, the theological, the metaphysical, and the positive, which John Mill held to throw such a clear light upon all history. But though the facts remain, the splendors of the fancy which surrounded them fade into the light of common day, and we find that in great part, at least, we have been like the astronomers who thought they were making scientific observations of the parallax, only to find that they had been measuring the error of their instruments. These visionary forms, these *Idola Speciis*, are not to be worshiped, but to

be strictly questioned, in order to know whether
there is any reality in them.

Foster. You do think, then, that there is
some reality in them?

The Squire. Yes; the universe of history, as
of everything else, has no doubt coherent laws;
but they require for their comprehension a
mind not less infinite than the universe itself.
I am reminded of the so-called Oriental tale of
the alchemist, who shows his disciple the universal solvent, which he has spent a lifetime in
obtaining, lying in a crucible; and the disciple
says, "O Sage, be not deceived; how can that
which is to dissolve all things be itself contained in a ladle!" Youth is the proper season for these finite ideals of life, and he who
knows the delight of them will desire that every
one should enjoy that season. But he is not
the less to be pitied to whom the experience of
age has not taught, as it taught Sir Isaac Newton, that we are but children on the shore, picking up here and there a pretty stone or shell,
while the great ocean of truth rolls its unex-
plored waters before us.

Foster. But the shells and the pebbles are
actual, and really rolled in by the sea.

The Squire. True. And if you will tell me
what you have now been picking up on the
beach of Persian history, I shall listen with
profit as well as pleasure.

Foster. I am a seeker, if not a finder, and I will content myself with stating some questions which have occurred to me on this subject. If they have a somewhat theological coloring, I may plead that if Gibbon the skeptic classed himself with the philosophers who held all religions to be equally false, Gibbon the historian recognized the important part which religion always plays in the history of nations. So I ask myself, Was there a relation between the greatness of the Persians, from the days of Cyrus through so many ages, and the national faith in a God of light and goodness, of which the sun was the fitting symbol, contending with the spirit of darkness and evil? Did some defect or degeneracy of their faith cause, as well as accompany, the break-up of the Persian empire at the end of the Sassanian dynasty? When the Arab conquest established the rule of the Caliphs on the ruins of the house of Sassan, and superseded the faith of Zoroaster by that of Muhammed, was this made possible, and even easy, because the proclamation of an absolute and irresistible Will was itself irresistible while its proclaimers heartily believed it? When the warlike and religious fervor of the new faith had cooled, was the skepticism of Omar Khayyám an instance, or only an accident, of the change? Did his learned studies at Nishapur in mathematics,

astronomy, and logic, joined with the recognition of the facts of other religions than their
own, make men skeptics, not only in religion,
but in politics? If so, how could men with
such a creed as Omar's resist the Tartar in-
vaders, those extraordinary savages, whose
utter cruelty of nature was again and again
transformed into gentleness and political wisdom by their hearty adoption of the faith in
God and his Prophet which its first promul-
gators had almost lost? Was not Sa'di one,
and probably the greatest, of the literary and
philosophical teachers of age after age of kings
and their subjects, of which teaching the ripest
fruits were seen in the reigns of the great
Mogul sovereigns of Agra and Delhi?

The Squire. I remember a discussion, some
fifty years ago, in this very room, between
Mountstuart Elphinstone and the old Bengal
civilian who then lived here. The latter asked
how it was that while the civilization of India
in the days of Akbar was in many respects
superior (as he held) to that of England in the
days of Elizabeth, Akbar's contemporary, the
one had been continually advancing ever since,
while the other had dwindled almost to nothing.
I ventured to suggest that the difference was the
difference between Christianity and Muhammedanism, and Elphinstone said he thought
so, too. But what of Hafiz, whom you just
now named with Omar and Sa'di?

Foster. I would rather hear about him from you. I am certainly out of my depth there.

The Squire. So am I; and so was Hafiz himself, as he is continually telling us. But what would you specially like to know?

Foster. Something of the poet, and something of the religious mystic, if such he was.

The Squire. The "Diwān," or Collection of the Odes of Hafiz, is a great book of songs arranged alphabetically, that is to say that the successive letters of the alphabet end the rhymes of successive sets of songs. These rhymes follow a different method from our own, or those of other European languages, there being only one rhyme, and that a double ending, for all the verses of each ode, though the words which supply all these rhymes are different from one another, as with us. The Persian metres, too, are more stately than our own, the proportion of long to short syllables, as I think, being much greater in that language than in ours. The words of the odes of Hafiz are most musical, and the thoughts and images to which they are wedded do not fall short of any standard of lyric poetry which we may supply: they are "simple, sensuous, and passionate" in the sense of Milton, and are successful attempts to make man's life harmonious in the sense of Carlyle. You will hardly think so from any of the translations you have found

in the library. I fancy our best chance would
be if we should ever have a translator like
Omar's Fitzgerald, who knows how to paraphrase when a literal version is impossible.
Failing something better, here is an attempt
of my own at such a version of his first
ode : —

> Bring out the wine, Cupbearer ! Ho !
>   Pour out, and high the goblet fill ;
> For though at first love smooth did flow,
>   Its course is crossed and troubled still.
>
> The zephyrs fragrance round us fling,
>   As through the Loved One's hair they play ;
> But for that fragrance which they bring
>   Our heart's blood is the price we pay.
>
> Spill wine upon the carpet spread
>   For prayer, should so the Teacher say ;
> For he by whom the march is led
>   Must know the customs of the way.
>
> There are who say that on this earth
>   A halting-place may still be found, —
> A halting-place for rest and mirth,
>   For those upon life's journey bound.
>
> But what of rest or mirth can tell
>   To me, who ever and anon
> Hear from each camel's tinkling bell,
>   " Load up ; the caravan goes on " ?
>
> The night is dark ; the waves strike fear :
>   The whirling waters how they roar !
> Our lot how should they know who bear
>   Their own light loads along the shore ?

Now all my work in vain has been :
    Self-seeking cannot come to good ;
The soul must find that good within,
    Not with the worldly multitude.

Hafiz, the Presence wouldst thou see,
    No moment's absence must thou know ;
When The Beloved hath met with thee,
    Give up the world, and let it go.

These verses may give you but little proof
of what I say ; but if you knew the original as
you do your Horace and Lucretius, you would
agree with me that not only for pathos, but for
singular felicity of expression, too, the warning
sound of the camel's bell may be compared
with the "*omnes codem cogimur*" of Horace, and
the contrast between the stormy sea and safe
shore with the "*suave mari magno*" of Lucretius.

Foster. I will take your comparison on trust,
till I get that opportunity of leisure and the
inclination to avail myself of it which the witty
author of "The Miseries of Human Life" says
it is so impossible to find. Meanwhile, let me
cap your Hafiz with a quotation from Sa'di
which caught my eye in turning over the pages
of Malcolm. Here it is : —

" Alas for him who is gone and has done no good deed !
The trumpet of march has sounded, and his load is not bound
    on."

The Squire. The beauty of the image is

brought out by the variations ; and the stern-
ness of the duty-loving Sa'di contrasts with the
gentle egotism of Hafiz. You may add another
parallel from the hopeless gloom of Omar,
which in Fitzgerald's version runs thus : —

> "'T is but a tent, where takes his one day's rest
> A Sultan to the realm of Death addrest ;
> The Sultan rises, and the dark Ferrash
> Strikes and prepares it for another Guest."

Foster. If this ode is a fair specimen of the
songs of Hafiz, it would seem easy to maintain
the mystical interpretation of his poetry. While
you were reciting it, I thought of one of Madame Guion's hymns. I forget the French, but
Cowper has translated it.

> "While place we seek or place we shun,
> The soul finds happiness in none ;
> But with a God to lead the way
> 'T is equal joy to go or stay."

The Squire. You may find many such paral-
lels between the odes of Hafiz and the hymns
of Madame Guion and other Christian mystics.
I once saw a letter to his friend from a young
Anglo-Indian, one of whom had turned, in ill-
ness, from the poetry of Sa'di and Hafiz to the
faith of Madame Guion and William Law, and
illustrated the doctrine of the Christian mystics
by a string of quotations from the Persian
poets. And it is related of Sir Gore Ouseley,
a great lover of Persian poetry, who was Eng-

lish ambassador to the Persian court early in this century, that when he was dying, long years after, he prayed in Persian. But I must confess that I have softened, and even concealed, the original by the word " Teacher," in the third stanza of this ode. It is, literally, " the chief of the Magians or infidel Fire-Worshipers," and this, again, is said to mean the keeper of the wine-shop: and I have given the Sufi interpretation of the name, which is that it signifies the spiritual teacher and guide of man through the hindrances of his earthly life which beset his entrance into the presence of God.

Foster. Can you give me a more precise account of these Sufis, and of the position of Hafiz among them?

The Squire. " I know when you do not ask me," as St. Augustine said of time. The facts are obscure, from their number and vastness; but I will tell you what little I know. With many differences, there is much likeness among the Hebrew prophets, the Christian monks, the Muhammedan dervishes, and the Buddhists of India. In times of religious fervor and earnestness, they have all more or less made good their claims to be men sent from God; in after days of national degeneracy, they have sunk into sensuality and hypocrisy, followed by more or less successful efforts at reformation.

Though the Koran does not approve of mo-
nasticism, and offers to the true believer mainly
the enjoyments of sense which come of fighting and of conquest, still there is a praise of
poverty and simplicity of life, and of absolute
prostration before the Divine Majesty, which
may have easily combined with the desire for
religious contemplation and for final absorp-
tion into God which came from the farther
East. And thence came the several orders of
dervishes in the Muhammedan tribes. When
the national life of Persia was roused to new
forms of energy by the successive invasions of
Arabs and Tartars, there were lovers of their
country, of whom Sa'di was the greatest example, who were the teachers of kings and
statesmen and people, and recluses vowed to
philosophy, poetry, and religious faith. The
right place for such men seemed to them to be
in the ranks of the dervishes, who were respected by the haughtiest kings, as the Christian monks were by our fierce princes in the
Middle Ages. The Sufis were, as I understand
it, ascetic and contemplation-loving reformers
among the dervishes. Sufi means " wool," and
the Sufis were so called because, like Shakespeare's Don Adriano de Armado, they " went
woolward for penance." Sa'di was a Sufi. So
was Hafiz, though he denounces the hypocrisy
of the sect.

Foster. This seems to me in favor of the religious interpretation of the songs of Hafiz. For how or why should he charge his brother dervishes with hypocrisy, if he himself was habitually practicing the same vice, and cloaking the mere love of sensual pleasures in language which the Sufis declared to be that of spiritual and religious devotion and ecstasy? Yet, after all, does not the sensuality seem as real as the spirituality, and is there any reconciliation or explanation of the contradiction?

The Squire. The contradiction is great and puzzling. The question was raised at the burial of Hafiz, when the rites of an orthodox Muhammedan were refused him till an augury had been taken (as the practice still is) from a verse of one of his odes, opened at hazard, and the words were found : —

" Turn not away from the bier of Hafiz,
For, though immersed in sin, he may yet be admitted into
    Paradise."

The dispute still continues, here no less than in Persia, and is settled by every man in accordance with his own taste or sentiment and estimate of the life of man. But perhaps some light may be thrown on it by the analogies in the schools of Greece and the Christian Church. The Socrates of the " Phædrus " and the " Symposium " is the very counterpart of the Sa'di of

the "Gūlistān" and "Būstān"; except that the
Persian believes in a personal relation between
man and his wise and beneficent Creator, a
belief not attributed to the Greek philosopher.
The Christian Church has always accepted an
interpretation of the Song of Solomon which
very closely resembles that which the Sufis
give of their songs of love and wine. I know
but little of the religious mysticism of the Middle Ages, but I believe there is much of it of
which the language, though not so sensual as
that of the Muhammedan Sufis, can only be
justified by interpreting as they do the enforced
asceticism and celibacy of the cloister, which,
while maintained by faith and prayer, would
give the intensity of suppressed earthly pas-
sions to the language of religious worship, and
especially in the adoration of the Virgin and
the saints. Then we know how these religious
fervors of devotion have often degenerated into
mere sensuality and hypocrisy, in sects and in
individuals. If we remember that the odes of
Hafiz probably spread over some fifty or sixty
years of his life, it may not be thought unreasonable to conjecture that they express very
various experiences and sentiments of his actual life. We read of his rivalry in love with
the prince of Shiraz, of his wife and his son,
and of his secluded and religious life as a dervish. Some have thought that traces of skep-

ticism at some period of his life may be found in his writings. The lovers of the higher criticism think that if we had the dates of the odes some further light might be thrown on the subject. But the chronological has been irrevocably merged in the alphabetical order; there is no evidence of what the actual life of Hafiz was at all or any periods of it; and we must be content to remain ignorant, unless we prefer the cloudland of conjecture.

Foster. Old Indians in the present day do not read and repeat Persian poetry as they did in the generation of which I suppose we may take Mountstuart Elphinstone as the representative?

The Squire. No; a great change was brought about in this respect by Lord Auckland's abolition of the use of Persian as the official language in all but diplomatic business.

Foster. How was that?

The Squire. Under the Mogul sovereigns, Persian was the language not only of the court, but of all government business, political, fiscal, and judicial.

Foster. Something, I suppose, like the use of Norman-French in England after the Conquest; with Arabic, like our Latin, in the background, for the church and law? And how does Hindustani come in?

The Squire. Hindustani, called in Persian

Urdū, or "the camp," in distinction from the
court, and the word from which we derive our
"horde," — this is the Hindi, or vernacular of
Hind, amplified by the introduction of Persian
and Arabic words, though retaining the Hindi
grammatical forms, becoming thus a *lingua
franca* for popular use beyond its proper limits.
With the other institutions of the Moguls we
took over the use of Persian in all official business, and the Munshi, or Persian secretary and
interpreter, became a part of the staff of the
English official in charge of political, revenue,
and judicial business. The language of business was soon discovered to be the language
of a new and fine literature ; and the volumes
on those shelves illustrate the enthusiasm which
the magistrates, judges, and collectors in our
older provinces, and our administrators in those
newly annexed, our political agents and resi-
dents in the native courts, and our military
officers threw into these studies from the time
when Warren Hastings set the example. But
then a generation of speculative reformers
arose, who asked why we should not act in the
spirit of the Moguls, and, instead of carrying on
their method with literal servility, make English
the official language, and so bring the several
nations of India into a new and more intimate
connection with our own literature and civilization. A retired Bengal judge expressed the

general opinion of practical men when he said
that you might as well make Sanskrit the official
language in the courts of Westminster as English in the administration of justice in India.
He, indeed, though a man of ability and eminence in the company's service, could see no
inconvenience in the employment of Persian in
the administration of justice; and such is the
force of habit that when he had occasion to
take notes of an important trial at the Somersetshire assizes, he actually wrote them in Persian rather than in the English words in which
the evidence was given, just as he had done,
many years before, when trying dakoits at
Jessore. But though the general opinion of
the native as well as the English officials was
against any change, Lord Auckland, by the
advice of Sir Charles Metcalfe, took what probably now seems to every one the obviously
reasonable course, and by his orders in 1837,
finally confirmed in 1838 by the home government, all official business was to be carried on
in the vernacular languages of the country.
Persian remained, and remains, the language
of diplomacy. It is not required in any other
branch of the public service; and it is not possible that men so hard-worked as our Indian
civilians and soldiers now are should find time
and energy for a purely literary study. They
all fall back on their Homer and Horace; or,

yet better, on their Shakespeare and Tennyson.
But enough of this ; you are, no doubt, already
silently quoting Horace against me, and repeating to yourself : —

"Persicos odi, puer, apparatus :
  Displicent nexæ philyra coronæ."

III.

THE OLD HALL AND THE PORTRAITS.

There stately dame and merry maid,
And Knight with visage stern,
By limner's cunning art portrayed,
Their eyes did on him turn.

OLD SONG.

As we opened the porch door, on coming back from a walk, we heard the sound of music. The children were dancing in the hall, — the squire's grandchildren, — led by their young aunt, not many years older than the eldest of them, while their mother played the piano. The hall still kept the main features of the old manor place which Leland had visited. Along the minstrel's gallery were hung breastplate, steel cap, sword, and other pieces of armor, — not, indeed, of Henry VIII.'s time, but of that of the Commonwealth. The dais was now level with the rest of the floor, and the bay window had become a porch; but the squint through which the lord could look into the hall, after he had withdrawn to the solar or parlor, might still be seen, though closed by the paneling on the other side, supposed to be the work

of Building Bess; and the lines of a huge
Tudor arch showed where the old fireplace had
been. The walls were hung with portraits
within a range of nearly three hundred years,
as the Squire had informed me. There was a
solemn brightness in his look as he watched the
dancers, and then glanced round the walls; and
he remarked, half to himself, " This makes an
old man feel young ; or indeed, not so much
young as undying, while the past and the future
are centred in the present, in one common life."

Foster. How many generations are there
now here ?

The Squire. Living, there are, as you see,
three, including myself ; in portraits of our
family, seven more. That small portrait on
panel, of William, Earl of Pembroke, Shakespeare's W. H., is perhaps rather earlier.

Foster. How does it come here ?

The Squire. There was some link of friendship between the Herbert family and that man
in Puritan bands and cloak, who was again connected with us.

Foster. I see the Puritan, and also a Cavalier with lace and velvet and flowing locks,
while each has by his side a lady, the two being
sisters, apparently.

The Squire. He was no Cavalier, in spite of
his dress, which indeed, as you know, was not
peculiar to the Cavaliers even in Charles I.'s

days. He is John Strachey, the friend to whom Locke writes from Holland with expressions of affection, and the prospect of talking over many things in "the parlour at Sutton." He died young, but the letters between the friends, which are still extant, show him to have been as enlightened as Locke himself. And I like to fancy that the armor still hanging there may have been worn by his father, who was serving with Locke's father in the regiment of Popham, their near neighbor in those parts. Strachey's grandfather framed, or helped to frame, the laws of the then newly settled colony of Virginia ; wrote verses prefixed to Ben Jonson's "Sejanus ; " and his account of the shipwreck of Sir George Summers, with whom he was at Bermuda, suggested some of the incidents of Shakespeare's "Tempest," taken either from his narrative, or, as the learned Mr. Furness thinks probable, from his own lips. The ladies are the great-granddaughters of Thomas Hodges, whose monument in the parish church of Wedmore, famous for King Alfred's treaty with the Danes, tells how he, " at the seige of Antwerpe, about 1583, with unconquered courage, wonne two ensigns from the enemy, where, receiving his last wound, he gave three legacies : his soule to his Lord Jesus ; his body to be lodged in Flemish earth ; his heart to be sent to his dear wife in England."

" Here lies his wounded heart, for whome
  One kingdom was too small a roome ;
  Two kingdoms, therefore, have thought good to part
  So stout a body and so brave a heart."

The old ladies with prayer-books are the mother and the grandmother of the young ladies
and of their husbands. And there, too, is
one whose name we know, but nothing more,
except that she died unmarried, while her portrait shows a true lover's knot, and a ring hung
round her neck. If the story was one of disap-
pointment and sadness, let us hope that there
were peace and contentment in the end.

Foster. Did you keep up your connection
with Virginia ?

The Squire. Yes. Two migrations are recorded in the family pedigree. And though the
male line has ended, I still correspond with a
worthy representative through the female line.
This gentleman opened a communication with
me after the war of 1861–65, in the troubles
of which he had lost his family pedigree, and
asked me to help him to supply its place ; and
in token of his claim he sent me photographs
of the pictures of several of our common an-
cestors, of which the counterparts are now
hanging before you. I have, too, a farther
connection with America, in which a literary
correspondence has ripened into warm personal friendship.

Foster. I remember the name of Henry Strachey in Mahon's "History of England" and Bancroft's "History of the United States," and in a publication of the New York Historical Society, called "The Treason of General Lee." Who was this Henry Strachey?

The Squire. There is his portrait, — a good one, by Northcote. When Lord Howe and Admiral Howe were sent out to put down the American patriots, Henry Strachey was sent with them as secretary to the commission. General Lee, a soldier of fortune, was the next in command under Washington, having so great a reputation that there had been some thought of giving the first command to him instead of to Washington. He was surprised and taken by Colonel Harcourt, and during his imprisonment proposed a scheme to the English commissioners for bringing back the country into complete submission to England, which Mr. Moore justly calls by the name of "treason." Although many important papers relating to American independence have been carried off from this house, we have still a large number of interesting documents connected with the period, as also with the negotiations for peace in 1782, the calendars of which fill several pages of the appendix to the sixth report of the Historical MSS. Commission of 1877. It was the same Strachey who negotiated the Peace of Versailles, which recognized the independence of the United States. I have papers of his, from the secret instructions of Lord Shelburne to the bills for post horses between Calais and Paris.

Foster. Why did Lord Shelburne send another envoy, when Oswald was already representing the British government in the negotiations?

The Squire. He had been instructed by Fox; and after Fox had retired from the ministry, on the death of Lord Rockingham, Shelburne, now become prime minister, sent Strachey to strengthen the hands of Oswald, whom he thought hardly a match for Franklin, Gay, and Adams, and who, in his anxiety for peace, "went before" the American commissioners, as Lord Shelburne expressed it. We have a story that Oswald had his papers ransacked while he was at the opera, and that Strachey, to avoid such a risk, always carried his in his pocket. In the archives at Washington there is a once secret diary of John Adams during these negotiations, in which he says, "Strachey is as artful and insinuating a man as they could possibly send; he pushes and presses every point as far it can possibly go; he has a most eager, earnest, pointed spirit." But the rivalry or hostility between Fox and Shelburne may have had something to do with the double

negotiations.   Fox was ready to give Shelburne
the character portrayed in the caricature of the
" Rolliad : " —

> " A noble Duke affirms, I like his plan:
>   I never did, my lords. I never can ;
>   Shame on the slanderous breath which dares instill
>   That I, who now condemn, advised the ill.
>   Plain words, thank Heaven, are always understood.
>   ' I could approve,' I said, but not ' I would.'
>   Anxious to make the noble Duke content,
>   My view was just to seem to give consent,
>   While all the world might see that nothing less was meant."

We have a tradition that when Lord Shelburne
was forming his ministry. Fox met Strachey
one Sunday afternoon in Hay Hill, and asked
him what he expected for himself, he being
then Secretary of the Treasury.   On his replying, " Lord Shelburne says I am to keep my
office." Fox rejoined, " Then, by God, you 're
out."   But Fox was wrong, for Shelburne
made Strachey an Under-Secretary of State,
and sent him, as I have said, to carry forward
the Versailles negotiations.

Foster. Lord Edmund Fitzmaurice, in his
" Life of Lord Shelburne," has clearly shown,
and history now recognizes, that Shelburne's
uncertain political action was not dishonesty,
but a Hamlet-like habit of looking too much
at all sides of every question.   It would be
harder to justify Fox's coalition with Lord
North.   But was not this Strachey also the

Indian secretary of Clive, whose fine portrait
by Dance you have here, and that seems to me
to be the original, of which I think there is
more than one replica? I remember that
Clive, in his defense before the House of Commons, said that, of the many services which
George Grenville had done him, none was
greater than that of recommending Henry
Strachey to him.

The Squire. Yes. And Dance's portrait corresponds with what we otherwise know of Clive.
He was coarse, unscrupulous, intolerant of
opposition, and, I think we must say, somewhat rapacious, though he himself "wondered
at his own moderation" when he looked back
on the treasures of Moorshedabad, of which
he did not appropriate the whole. But he was
also of political as well as military genius ; and
he did not hesitate to set public above private
interests, as when he declared war against the
Dutch in India, at a moment in which they
held the bills which represented his whole fortune ; and he was capable of warm and faithful
friendship. He was a sort of Bismarck.

Foster. What a number of false accounts
of his death there have been, from the contemporary letters of Horace Walpole and the
sayings of Dr. Johnson down to "Notes and
Queries," only a year or two ago, which I think
you have more than once written to set right!

The Squire. I took down my account from the mouth of the late Sir Henry Strachey, who had it from his mother, who was in the house at the time. Clive suffered, till he would endure it no longer, from a painful disease, of which he says, in a letter which I have : " How miserable is my condition ! I have a disease which makes life intolerable, but which my doctors tell me will not shorten it one hour."

Foster. You spoke of Clive's political genius ; you attribute to him the foundation of our Indian empire, the expansion of which has been equaled by its stability, — a stability which could, at the end of a hundred years, stand such a test as the mutiny of 1857.

The Squire. After Clive had defeated Suraj-oo-Dowlah, and set up Meer Jaffier in his place, he left the East India Company's factory at Calcutta to carry on their trade, as before, under a native, though now not only friendly but subservient prince. But the sudden acquisition of such enormous wealth by Clive and his colleagues in that war had excited a mad lust for a like acquisition of wealth by the company's servants left by Clive in the management of the Bengal factory. The East India Company in Leadenhall Street allowed each of its servants in Bengal to carry on some private trading for himself, and now, in defiance of the opposition of the governor, Vansittart, who was, if I remember rightly, supported by no one but young Warren Hastings, they converted this private trade into a system of mere extortion and robbery of the Nawab and his subjects. Meer Jaffier was superseded by Cossim Ali, whom they hoped to make a more subservient tool; but he, too, after efforts at conciliation which it is quite pathetic to read of, was obliged to make a stand for the rights of his people. War began, and the directors at home, alarmed at the danger of a return to a state of things like that from which Clive's victory at Plassey had saved them, sent him out again, in 1765, to restore order. He reinstated Meer Jaffier in the Nawabship; but he saw that the relations of the company to the native rulers of Bengal had become so changed that they could no longer be merely those of merchants trading in a foreign country, but must of necessity give those merchants a share in the political government of that country. Under the Mogul sovereigns, the diwan, or collector of the revenues, shared some branches of the civil government of the province with the Nawab, and Clive, by obtaining from the Mogul emperor the office of diwan for the company, made that beginning of political responsibilities, as well as rights, which was to lay the foundations of our future empire in India.

Foster. What were the next stages of the structure raised on this foundation?

The Squire. The Mogul empire was in ruins. It is always best to keep old forms as far as possible, and to make the new life seem at least to grow out of them, though it can no longer be infused into them. It is our English way, and Clive took it when he obtained the diwanee from the sovereign who had still the nominal right to grant it. But the government by the Nawab, of which it was the complement, had become little more than a sham ; and, under Warren Hastings, this, too, was absorbed into the English rule in Bengal, because Hastings found that in no other way was any tolerable administration of justice possible. But there was no resting here. As the once strong empire of the Moguls fell to pieces, the general anarchy gave opportunity for the rise of that terrible race of conquerors and plunderers, the Mahrattas. Hastings saw that the British territory must be overrun, and perhaps swallowed up in its turn, by these locusts, if no adequate defense were provided, and he resorted to the alliance with the Nawab of Oude which led to the Rohilla war, which he held to be defensible in honor and justice no less than by expediency. His object was to interpose a strong native state between the Mahrattas and the British province. If the Rohilla chiefs had been faithful to their treaty with Oude, Hastings would have supported their alliance; but when the Rohillas opened their country to the Mahrattas for the invasion of Oude, which must have been followed by that of Bengal, he held himself called on by expediency, while not forbidden by good faith and honor, to give the Nawab of Oude effectual support in the conquest of the Rohillas, who in fact had no right but that of recent conquest.

Foster. After the complete vindication of Hastings by Sir James Stephen and Sir John Strachey from the charges brought against him, they can hardly be renewed by any future historian: but it is very difficult to understand how those charges could have been made by Burke, more or less sanctioned by Pitt, and adopted as true history by Mill and Macaulay.

The Squire. It is difficult. They had before them all the evidence that we have now, if they chose to examine it; and not one of them, whether as statesman or historian, had any right to make and maintain such charges without such examination. It seems to me no justification, nor even excuse for Burke, to say that he was carried away by his hatred of injustice and oppression, and sympathy with the oppressed, and that he thus became the victim of the malignity of Francis, and of his own imagination and rhetoric. Such excuses may serve an ill-informed private person, but not a great statesman and leader of men. The same may be said of Pitt, if he believed the charges, as he said ; while still more unworthy of him are the suggestions that he was willing to let the opposition waste their energies on such a subject, and that he was jealous of the favor which Hastings received from the king and the chancellor. James Mill I knew, and his treatment of Hastings, though fatal to the character of an accurate and impartial historian, is less hard to explain. His disposition was, like that of Francis, malignant. Coulson asked Peacock of him, " Will he like what I like, and hate what I hate ? " and Peacock replied, " No, he will hate what you hate, and hate what you like." His temper was eminently destructive. He did some good service in the pulling down and destroying of much that was utterly corrupt and bad in our political and social condition, but when good and evil were intermixed he saw only the evil ; and he habitually imagined it even where it did not exist. Above all, he hated all men in authority. When he wrote his history of India, he was prepared to see the government of India by the company and its servants in the worst possible light. No historian is really and completely impartial ; he necessarily collects his materials in the light of some preconceived theory or plan. Those

extracts from the evidence as to the government of Hastings, which are now shown to be
garbled by separation from their suppressed
context, no doubt seemed to him the salient
parts, because they supported his foregone conclusions ; and he was probably unconscious of
dishonesty when he afterwards marshaled and
embodied them in his history. While we condemn his want of impartiality and the want of
wisdom in his reflections, we must not overlook
the skill with which he compressed the substance
of a volume into a few pages, or the brilliancy
with which he described a battle. Then as to
Lord Macaulay, the actual working of the
judicial code which he compiled and con-
structed for India has proved him to be a great
jurist ; but now that the glamour of his rhetoric
has faded into the light of common day, and
we see him as he is, we know that he was the
most brilliant of rhetoricians, that his great acquaintance with books was always made subservient to his imagination and his rhetoric,
and that his gorgeous essays on Clive and
Hastings in particular are merely imaginative
reproductions from the pages of Mill, and with
no authority beyond his.   It is a pity that such
wealth of historical imagination as Lord Macaulay possessed was not more wisely husbanded
and expended by him for the benefit of others ;
for without the help of the historical imagination
no real study of history is possible.

Foster. I dare say you remember the dignified but friendly expostulation of Sir William Jones in reply to Burke's insolent threat that, if he heard of his siding with Hastings, he would do everything in his power to get him recalled? The letter is characteristic of the writer, — kind-hearted, genial, learned, overflowing with intellectual activity, and a love of display of all these merits which is pleasing from its simplicity.

The Squire. Chaucer's description of the Sergeant of the Law still suits the great lawyer even to his love of display, — *étalage*, as the French call it : —

> " No where so busy a man there n'as,
> And yet he seemed busier than he was."

Foster. And how gracefully he turns his expostulation into a compliment, declaring that if he was ever unjustly attacked (as in fact Burke had threatened to attack him), he was sure that his friend would pour, in his defense, the mighty flood of his eloquence, like Ἀσσυρίου ποταμοῖο μέγας ῥόος ! The letter is in the third volume of Burke's correspondence, edited by Lord Fitzwilliam ; but where does the Greek come from? I have looked in vain for it.

The Squire. From Callimachus's " Hymn to Apollo." The passage runs thus : —

Ἀσσυρίου ποταμοῖο μέγας ῥόος, ἀλλὰ τὰ πολλὰ
λύματα γῆς καὶ πολλὸν ἐφ' ὕδατι συρφετὸν ἕλκει.

While we talked, the children left off dancing, and stayed playing in the hall, while the two ladies joined us as listeners. The younger now said to her father, " What does that mean ? You know, father, that you do not send me to Girton or Somerville Hall."

The Squire replied gravely, —

> " ' Madam, the sentence of this Latin is,
> Woman is mannes joy and mannes bliss.' "

" But," rejoined the young lady, " Mr. Foster has just said that the words are Greek ; and though Greek of Girton 'is to me unknowe,' you have taught me to understand Chanticlere's Latin translation."

The Squire. Well, the sentence of the Greek, in such English as I can muster, is : —

> " Great is the flow of the Assyrian river ;
> But on its waters it brings down much filth,
> The offscouring of the land."

There is at least this resemblance between the quotations of Chanticlere and Sir William Jones, that each of these polite gentlemen conveys a reproof in the guise of a compliment ; and I can tell you a story which shows that the latter, no less than the former, enjoyed the humor of his covert allusion. My uncle told me that, when he was a young Bengal civilian, he went with some of his fellows to dine with Sir William Jones. After dinner, the judge told them of his having received from Burke a most unbecoming message of threats of what he would do if he heard that he (Sir William Jones) dared to side with Hastings. " But," he went on, " I answered him by sending him these lines from Callimachus." Here he repeated some Greek lines, and continued : " Perhaps you may not remember them " (" Of course," interposed my uncle, " we had never heard of them "), " but their purport is this : 'The Euphrates is a noble river, but it rolls down all the dead dogs of Babylon to the sea.' "

Foster. Rather a free translation, but very terse and epigrammatic.

The Squire. Yes ; and while the latent irony in the four Greek words of compliment in the letter is revealed in their context, it is an irony so fine that if Burke recalled the context he could hardly have resented it. And then we have the good judge quietly enjoying his own wit and learning, while he told his young guests the real meaning of his quotation. I ought to tell you that this dinner-table incident must have been eight or nine years after the date of the letter.

Foster. Though Sir William Jones lived before Bopp and Max Müller and the age of scientific philology, his Oriental learning, resting on his classical and modern European scholarship, must have had a great influence

on those young men who went out from school
at the age of fifteen or sixteen, or even earlier,
to spend their lives in India, in the civil or
military service of the company.

The Squire. I think and read of the men of
that generation with ever new wonder and admiration alike for their moral and their intellectual virtues. As I remarked just now, the
conduct of the company's servants in India
after Clive left, in 1760, was infamous. Under
Clive's second administration, followed by that
of Hastings, there was considerable improvement, while under the governorship of Cornwallis and Sir John Shore both the services
rose to that high condition and character which
they have ever since maintained, and which I
believe have seldom been equaled in the history of the world for incorruptibility, high-
mindedness, and commanding genius in all the
arts of peace and war ; and all this with a corresponding love of letters and literary culture.

Foster. The personal character and influence of Lord Cornwallis and Sir John Shore
must have had a good deal to do with this general devotion of character.

The Squire. No doubt. I remember the
younger Charles Buller saying to me that his
father, a Bengal civilian of that time, was not
a man of specially high sentiment, but that in
any doubtful question he would have been sure

to ask himself, "What would Lord Cornwallis have thought of it?" And what a meaning and force there must have been in the words of Sir John Shore to my own father when he first came to India, — "Don't call them 'black fellows.'" Mountstuart Elphinstone arrived in India just as Cornwallis was leaving it; but in him we have the very flower and fruit of this period in the highest perfection. When the young civilian rode all through the bloody battle of Assaye by the side of General Wellesley, the Duke of Wellington that was to be, and at the storming of Gawalgarh, the latter said that Elphinstone had mistaken his vocation, which should have been that of a soldier. But he soon showed himself equally fitted for the work of a diplomatist, in the midst of the intricacies of the policy of Lord Wellesley in its contention with that of the Mahrattas. In the negotiations which ended by his cutting a way with his little force through the army of the Peishwa at Poonah, he showed himself alike a diplomatist and a soldier. In the reorganization of the central provinces and as governor of Bombay, — and he would have been governor-general, had his health allowed, — he proved himself to be no less able as an administrator and a ruler of men. And you must not forget his literary culture and love of books, Greek and Latin, English and Italian, which supplied him with

examples of action as well as language in which
to describe it ; while his Persian studies awakened sentiments deeper than those of the classical poets, and at the same time gave him, as
it had given Hastings, the great practical advantage of being able to conduct the business
of the hour with the native statesmen in their
own diplomatic language.   The life of Elphinstone, as told by Colebrooke, and again by
Cotton, has all the charm of a romance, and
yet it is the record of an actual life of hard
work.   I knew him well; as my father's lifelong friend he was the hero of my boyish imagination, and after his return from India till his
death I shared in that affectionate friendship
by which he endeared himself to all who knew
him.   At Assaye, Gawalgarh, and Poonah he
showed himself to be " worthy," in Chaucer's
sense of the word ; and in every other respect
he realized Chaucer's ideal of " a very perfect
gentle knight."   He was " in his port as meek
as is a maid," — meek in his unaffected humility; and indeed you may take Chaucer's description, word by word, and you will find the
counterpart in Elphinstone as he actually was.

Foster. You remind me of Elphinstone's
own eulogy on Sir Barry Close, and of the
lament of Sir Bors over the body of Sir Launcelot.   But what is your judgment of the Indian
policy of Lord Wellesley?

The Squire (pointing to a full-length portrait of a soldier). If that man could come down and speak, he could answer your question better than I can.

Foster. The portrait looks like a Romney, but who is the man?

The Squire. He is Colonel William Kirkpatrick, another of those men of action and of culture of whom we were just now talking. He was first military, and then political secretary to Lord Wellesley; and it is said that when Lord Wellesley (then Lord Mornington), on his way out, found him on sick leave at the Cape, his plans of policy were materially modified, or even changed, by what he learned from Kirkpatrick. Lord Wellesley may have been as ambitious and unscrupulous as Mill depicts him; but when I contrast the condition of the two hundred and fifty millions of men, women, and children under British rule or influence at the present day with the terrible devastation and misery under which all India lay while the power of the Mahrattas and the Pindarees remained unbroken, I am very little inclined to condemn a policy which did so much to carry forward the beneficial work which was not possible without the destruction of those powers of evil.

Foster. Who is that man in the naval uniform of the last century, over Clive's portrait?

The Squire. Admiral Watson, who took Clive's force from Madras to the Hoogly, and supported his military operations in Bengal. His name always reminds me of an instance of the difference of an incident as related by the dignified Muse of History and as told by Jack to Harry as it actually happened. In Orme and other historians you will find that Admiral Watson assisted the operations for the attack on Calcutta by landing a party of sailors from the ships ; but it has come to me in tradition that "Old Benn" (a member of the Calcutta factory, and afterwards Sir John Walsh, by virtue of the sign manual) told young Harry, "We sent to Watson to let us have some of his sailors, and he answered, ' I will send the men, but don't make jackasses of them.' Now, the very thing we wanted them for was to make jackasses of them ;" that is, to drag up the guns.

Foster. Is that bit of paper with some minute writing on it, which I see in a glass case, one of your Indian relics ?

The Squire. You can hardly read it without a magnifying-glass, but it is a letter from my father's half-brother, Robert Latham, to his mother, from the prison of Hyder Ali at Bangalore. Latham was a Madras civilian, who volunteered for service in the war with Hyder. He was in Colonel Baillie's detachment, and was among the survivors of that desperate contest of so many hours, against overwhelming numbers, which Mill has so graphically described. They endured a rigorous imprisonment in irons for three years and a half. This letter could reach its destination only by being, as you see, so written that it could be conveyed secretly out of the prison, inclosed in a quill.

Foster. I remember that the correspondence between the governor-general and Elphinstone, in those last days of his residency with the Peishwa at Poonah, had to be carried on by quills. But does Latham tell much of his imprisonment?

The Squire. We have his story after he was again free; but there is something pathetic in the fact that this letter from the poor fellow tells nothing of his imprisonment except that he had then been eighteen months in chains, but of the grief with which he thinks of his want of love and duty to his mother in his past life. She was a stern woman, although very kind to her grandchildren, of whom I was one. But, stern as she was, we may hope that she did not receive this letter with the hardness recorded of the mother of another of those prisoners of Hyder, of whom it is told that when she heard that her son was chained to a fellow-prisoner, she only observed, "The man who's chained to our Davie will have a gey time of it."

Foster. Hurrell Froude said that a country
house was of use because it was a place where
you could keep things which you did not like to
destroy, though they were not worth preserv-
ing ; but I should rather say, where you can
keep things worth keeping, but which would,
without its help, be destroyed.

The Squire. I often think so. This old house
is of no importance in itself, — it is no Long-
leet or Hatfield, — yet it touches the main
course of English history, from the time of
Edward the Confessor to the present day, at
many minute points. The little brook which
you see there from the terrace has no name,
and it runs into a river not known out of the
county ; but that stream runs into the Avon,
and the Avon into the Severn, which pours the
waters of its smallest tributaries into the Atlantic with its own. And so long as the old
walls remain there will be two or three persons
in each generation in whom they will awaken
and keep alive a sense of the reality of English
history which cannot be got by books alone.

Foster. Then do such thoughts make you
say, when you look at these portraits, as
the monk said to Wilkie when looking on Titian's Last Supper in the Escurial, "These seem
to me the real men, and we the shadows " ?

The children were still playing in the hall.
The Squire looked at them and at his daughters,

and answered : " I can hardly agree with the old monk, while I have these witnesses to the reality and the worth of our actual life. Yet his words were not without meaning."

Then the elder lady went back to the piano, and played and sang "The Fine Old English Gentleman," while her sister joined in the refrain. Their eyes met those of their father ; and he smiled approvingly, but I fancied with more thought of the singers than of the song, though he liked that, too.

IV.

A GENERAL ELECTION : RIGHT AND WRONG IN POLITICS.

Men of Somerset! Arouse you!
With the vote the law endows you;
Claim the right the law allows you,
Hear your Country's call!

ELECTION SONG.

THE stir of a general election broke in upon the usual quiet of the old manor house. The Squire's eldest son was a candidate for one of the divisions of the county. The rooms in the old tower were turned into offices, in and out of which flowed daily streams of election business. There were committee-men, canvassers, and wire-pullers to talk and be talked to; addresses; notices of meetings; leaflets, serious and comic; new songs set to old popular tunes; photographs of the handsome young candidate, with his address on the back, to be sent to every elector; and then, as the great day drew on, the thousands of cards to be sent by post, one to every voter, with his name and number and polling-place, and a facsimile of the ballot paper, with an explanation how it

should be used. The candidate's wife, zealous
alike for her husband and for the cause he
represented, helped as only a woman can help
in such work, rousing a new enthusiasm as
often as the crowd met the carriage in which
she sat by her husband's side, or as she came
into the meeting with him, while hundreds of
voices joined in the " March of the Men of
Somerset " or " Wait till the Polling-Day." The
candidate himself, while ably supported by the
leading men of his party, understood his own
work well, from his experience in county business, in which he had for some years taken an
active part. The Squire wrote leaflets and
songs, and took the chair at such of the meetings as were within his reach ; and I thought
myself fortunate in this my first opportunity of
seeing both the serious and the humorous side
of a general election. The humor was for the
most part, but not always, good humor. The
" civil dudgeon " sometimes " grew high, and
men fell out, they knew not why ; " or at least
when they would have found it hard to explain
why. At one of the meetings to which I went
with my friends, a sound like that of carpet-
beating, at the further end of the hall, made us
on the platform wonder whether the wielders
of the sticks were not Irishmen, instead of the
young farmers they seemed to be. At another
meeting, the candidate's brother stood for an

hour apparently speaking, but with no sound
from his mouth being audible. On still another evening, there were ominous signs that
our opponents had packed the meeting, and
might be expected to storm the platform, when
a sturdy farmer arrived with what Mrs. Quickly
would have called "a rescue or two," and
which, with strategical skill, he formed into a
wedge, with a chimney-sweep with brush and
bag at its point. No one dared face the infinite possibilities of that brush, and the foe
was scattered. But our side was generally the
popular one; and on one occasion I was
amused at seeing our assailants driven to take
refuge behind the candidate's wife, as she sat
fearless on the platform, while they tried to
assure her it was for her own safety that they
begged her to escape with them through a
window six feet from the ground. But for the
most part these meetings, of which we had
sometimes three in one evening, and often in
the open air, as the time was summer, were
not only friendly, but enthusiastic, as they
consisted chiefly of our own party. And I was
much struck with the seriousness of the people,
enthusiastic as they were; men, and women
too, were so evidently desiring to understand
the arguments of the speakers, and to learn
from what they heard.

The writ had come down to the sheriff, the

nomination had been made, and the eve of the polling-day had arrived.

"Venit summa dies, et ineluctabile fatum."

At night I went with the Squire and his youngest son and daughter to a last meeting, while our candidate and his wife went to another. The enthusiasm was great, yet I saw something serious as well as earnest in the faces before me. We knew that other meetings were being held that night, and that another host was mustering for the morrow, arrayed against us, with hopes no less high than our own. A solemn feeling of suspense, and even of awe, fell upon me, and I doubt not on those with me ; and though the battle was to be fought with ballot papers in orderly polling-places, I could not but think that as great issues might be at stake as were at Agincourt, and that there was no unfitness in recalling as I did the words of Shakespeare : —

> " From camp to camp through the foul womb of night
> The hum of either army stilly sounds,
> That the fixed sentinels almost receive
> The secret whispers of each other's watch.
> Fire answers fire, and through their paly flames
> Each battle sees the other's umber'd face ;
> Steed threatens steed, in high and boastful neighs
> Piercing the night's dull ear, and from the tents
> The armourers, accomplishing the knights,
> With busy hammers closing rivets up,
> Give dreadful note of preparation."

Then followed that long day of eager hopes
and fears and guesses at what must remain unknown till the morrow, while the rival candidates and their wives spent the day in visiting
every polling-place. They once or twice met
and crossed each other, with the courtesy which
seldom fails English gentlefolk under such circumstances.

I am not old enough to recall, but the Squire
has described to me, the days when the free-
holders journeyed from every end of the county
to their county town, there to choose two knights
of the shire by acclamation at the hustings, or,
if need were, by voting, presided over by the
sheriff, who kept the poll open day after day,
and even week after week, as long as there
was a single voter to come in. The several
forms, ending with that of the two chosen
knights, girded with swords, riding in procession at the head of their supporters, were probably little changed from the days of Hamden,
or perhaps even of Simon de Montfort ; and
though the counties had been divided, and
other polling-places added to that of the county
town, the main proceedings were still the same,
as the Squire has told me, before the passing
of the Ballot Act. On the hustings, a great
wooden structure erected in the open air, the
High Sheriff presided over a crowd of the free-
holders and the larger tenants of the county.

The Queen's writ was read ; the names of the rival candidates were proposed one after another, with the shouts of their several supporters. As nothing turned on the decision of the sheriff, he might be pardoned if he looked to the side of his own party and declared that their ayes had it. His decision was challenged, and the day for the polling appointed. My friend gave me an account of his doings, both as county magistrate and as party committeeman, in his own village, during one such polling-day. There was a polling-place in the village, and his story was this : —

A few days before, there had been something of an election riot in a large town some ten miles off, and a timid householder in the village, having taken it into his head that the rioters would now march upon his village, made oath to that effect, and demanded the appointment of special constables. The justices could not refuse the demand, and the Squire had to swear in the constables, and to provide them with staves, for which the county had afterwards to pay a bill of twenty pounds. A strong body of rural police was also marched in. Their superintendent told my friend — the only magistrate there — that, in the event of a riot, the special constables would be of no use if they were at the time dispersed among the crowd, and that they must be kept together in

a body, in case they should be wanted to act.
So he locked them all up in the parish school-
room; they meekly submitting to an order
which possibly the magistrate had no legal
power to enforce. He sent them in some old
newspapers, and all the bread and cold meat
which the committee of the rival candidates
had left unconsumed in the several public
houses; and so they were left, losing their
votes and their share in the general fun, till
the polling-day was over. The polling-booth
was a wooden shed set up on a bit of open
ground in the middle of the village, with a
shelter for the officers and their books, — a
shelter luckily not wanted, as the day proved
to be one of bright autumn weather. The
church clock struck eight, and the Squire, who
was a keen party politician no less than an active magistrate, was the first to give his vote.
The incredible muddle-headedness of voters,
which is now hid from all but the presiding
officer and the personation agent, who sit in
secret conclave in the polling-room, could then
be witnessed and laughed at in open day.
There, for instance, was a freeholder who had
never heard of the House of Commons, but
whose father had turned a bit of roadside waste
into a freehold by building a house upon it,
and living there without disturbance from the
parish overseers. He had been brought up by

the zealous agent of one party, but was now clutched at by him of the other side. When asked for whom he voted, he could only look scared and say that he was a stoutish gentleman with a bald head, but he did not rightly remember his name. And then when the polling-clerk, who had at first forbidden the rival agents to interfere, did at last reluctantly say that each might tell the voter the names of their respective candidates, the poor bewildered man replied again and again, "That's not the name," till all were exhausted ; but then, after there was no other to come, he thought it was the last which he had heard, and so voted, to his own relief and that of every one except the discomfited agent. There were no telegrams in those days, but a mounted messenger came in every hour from headquarters only to report to the Squire's committee that they were losing everywhere, and to carry back the like bad report from them. Still they put a good face on the matter, and kept their own counsel, in spite of the eager inquiries from the other side, who for some reason had not provided for keeping themselves informed of their own success. The last incident which the Squire told me of was a report to his committee of two voters still left in an outlying village. An omnibus was chartered in hot haste ; the voters were brought in before the clock struck four, and one voted on one side, and one on the other. Then the special constables were set free from a custody which had been inflicted on none but themselves ; the crowd of voters and non-voters dispersed in good humor, though still in ignorance of how the day had gone ; and my friend went home to learn the full account of the utter beating his party had received.

But these are memories of an almost forgotten past. Now all these things are shrouded, by the secrecy of the ballot, in a silence which becomes, as I have said, solemn and almost awful to those to whom the election is a serious interest, as the polling-day goes on. At last, then, night had fallen on the fight, which was lost and won, though no one knew how the day had gone. Next morning the counting began in the Court House of the principal town in the division. The sheriff who presided had given me permission to be among the favored few who were allowed to be present during the counting. These were the candidates and their wives and their agents and the officials who had to count. The seals of the several ballot boxes were examined and broken, and the number of voting papers in each was verified ; then the whole were thrown together, " made hay of," and finally separated according to the names of the candidates for which they were marked. This separation went on at four tables at once ; and as each packet of one hundred papers was completed, it was filed with a blue or a red label, as that candidate's color might be, by the counting clerk, and then handed by him to the agent of the opposite side. If he was satisfied with it, he handed it to the other agent, who made a like examination ; and if there was — as sometimes happened — a doubt as to the meaning of the voter's mark, or any other question as to the reception of the ballot paper, the point was decided by the sheriff. An equal number of red and of blue labels lay on the table, for tying up the successive packets of a hundred ballot papers for one or the other candidate. The keen eyes of our candidate's wife were the first to discover that the wrappers of her husband's color were exhausted, while several remained on the other side. The counting was soon finished ; the numbers were called out in the room ; and the sheriff proceeded to announce the result to the eager crowd which was waiting outside. Our candidate was elected by a majority of seven hundred and ninety-three votes ; and the declaration of the poll was received with enthusiastic shouts by his supporters, while those who were there in the hope of another result slipped silently away. The defeated candidate was not the old member, nor of his party, but the important question had been whether the constituency had, or

had not, changed from its old political faith.
There could be no doubt that the popular feeling, in so far as it could be shown by public
meetings, was in my friend's favor, but nothing
but the actual poll could tell the opinion of the
silent voter, who did not go to the meetings
on either side. To borrow Burke's simile, till
then we had heard the voice of the noisy grass-
hoppers, but the stately cattle were browsing
in silence. Now the newly elected M. P. knew
that a majority of both were for him. He had
to return thanks again and again to the crowd
who accompanied him from the town hall to
his hotel, from the hotel to the railway station.
The carriage in which he and his wife sat was
drawn — "hauled," as the country people call
it — by their enthusiastic supporters through a
crowd which numbered thousands, and covered
perhaps a mile of ground. We were half an
hour in reaching the station, out of which the
train could hardly make its way. It was a
triumphal progress, for the new M. P. was already well known in his county.

The old Squire, with his younger children
and his grandchildren, had waited at home for
the telegram which was to tell how the battle
had gone. The news had been telegraphed in
various other directions. And when we — for
I had returned with the new M. P. and his
wife — reached the station where our carriage

was waiting for us, we were welcomed by a band of music heading a procession gathered from many miles around. The horses were taken out, and the carriage was "hauled" by the enthusiastic crowd through the village, and so up to the old manor house. The people had of their own accord put up triumphal arches. The Squire's younger children and grandchildren, after hanging out a great flag on the tower, and smaller ones at every window, had joined the procession on its road; and it at last entered the gateway through the old battlemented wall, led by some of the principal tenants, while the band played "Auld Lang Syne," and the Squire stood at the door to welcome his son and his son's wife. It was a grand sight. I shall be told, and shall grant, that it is common enough on such occasions; but if I am asked why, then, it seems so striking, I answer that it was a grand sight, and a sight to awake our deepest thoughts and feelings, to see that multitude of faces of men, women, and children, full of gladness and of love for those whom they were rejoicing to honor while sharing their triumph. It was, and from its nature must be, a passing enthusiasm, but it was not the less real for all that; the brightness of the moment must soon fade into the light of common day, but all had been the better as well as the happier that even for a moment they had

been raised above themselves ; and to many it
would be a memory that would never die.
The Squire and his son each said a few words
of thanks, which were heartily responded to.
The shadows of evening were falling as the
band again struck up "Auld Lang Syne," and
the people slowly filed through the archway ; when the last had disappeared we went
slowly into the house, and I heard the old
Squire repeat to himself, "Nunc Dimittis."

The newly elected knight of the shire went to
London to take his seat at the meeting of
Parliament, and the Squire and I walked down
the avenue and sat again under the shade of
Berowne's oak, while the gentle splashing of
the little waterfall sounded in our ears, and accompanied without disturbing our talk. The
Squire had been laughing at some rather strong
abuse of his son in the local paper which
represented the defeated party ; but as I fancied that he might possibly be more annoyed
than he allowed, I said : —

"It is really too bad that a respectable
newspaper should make such grossly false
statements as to the moral and intellectual
unfitness of the successful candidate, and of
his election having been due to promises impossible of fulfillment, and to every other kind
of influence which could be exercised over
what they now call an ignorant electorate."

The Squire. That is nothing to what the losing party always says, though without rushing into print, in such days of excitement as follow a contested election. It is pretty Fanny's way; and the man who wins can afford to say with the navvy, when they laughed at him because his wife beat him, " It amuses her, and it does not hurt me."

Foster. I should say " ugly Fanny " and her ugly way. I cannot help feeling more annoyed than you seem to be.

The Squire. I am older, and therefore tougher than you. When men get upon politics, they should allow each other the liberty which each claims for himself, of using words in a parliamentary sense, as the phrase goes. If a correspondent subscribes himself your obedient humble servant, you do not therefore expect him to wait on you at dinner, or carry your portmanteau to the station. Lord St. Leonards, in his " Handy Book on Property Law," says that, though the Court of Chancery will enforce the terms of any contract, it will not hold a vendor to be bound by what it calls the babble of the auction-room. The language at an election, like that at an auction, though it may be in the way of blame instead of praise, is high-flown, exaggerated, and has a conventional meaning which it does not bear in ordinary life. I do not defend it ; I am sorry for

it, and wish it could be avoided, especially as I
know that some people do more or less accept
such language in its ordinary sense, and so
become embittered in feeling, whether they
believe the abuse to be true or know it to be
false. There is plenty of evil in the world. I
am sorry for it, but cannot help it. I know
that the day may be rainy and the road muddy;
but there is plenty of sunshine, too, and we
shall get to our journey's end, if we do not
mind being splashed with mud and getting a
little wet on the way. Or you may change the
metaphor, and say with the book of Proverbs,
"Where no oxen are, the crib is clean: but
much increase is by strength of the ox."

Foster. Though I shall be arguing against
myself, I can cap your quotation with a passage which I lighted upon in a pamphlet in the
library, the other day, and which I think I
remember: "The free expression of opinion,
as our experience has taught us, is the safety
valve of passion. That noise when the steam
escapes alarms the timid; but it is the sign
that we are safe." And again: "I have lived
now for many years in the midst of the hottest
and noisiest of the workshops of constitutional
freedom, and have seen that amidst the clatter
and the din a ceaseless labor is going on; stub-
born matter is reduced to obedience, and the
brute powers of society, like the fire, air, water,

and minerals of nature, are, with clamor, indeed, but also with might, educated and shaped into the most refined and regular forms of usefulness for man." [1]

The Squire. You have a capital memory, and the whole passage is worthy of Milton or Burke. The Old Parliamentary Hand was young when he wrote that; but fifty years' experience has evidently only confirmed him in his beliefs. So far as my own observation goes, I should say that the fastidious and sensitive men, who try to keep aloof from the dust and din, and still baser elements of politics, and try to rise above party, always, in practice, sink below it. The only men whom I have known to rise above party are those who, with moral and intellectual earnestness, throw themselves sometimes into one, and sometimes into the other party, as either seems to them right or wrong. That state of negation which the non-party man attains to is, in practice, a dull, half-hearted conservatism, as far inferior to the true conservatism as to the true liberalism. Think, too, of the unconscious selfishness of these men, who live in the enjoyment of all the infinite blessings of civilization, and have no words except of censure and contempt for those by whose hard work, with all its

[1] *Letter to the Right Rev. W. Skinner, D. D., on the Functions of Laymen in Church*, by W. E. Gladstone.

begriming incidents, and by that alone, all
those blessings have been won and are still
secured for them. "For us was thy back so
bent, for us were thy straight limbs and fingers so deformed; thou wert our conscript, on
whom the lot fell, and, fighting our battles,
wert so marred."

Foster. Our conversation is getting to be as
full of quotations as the play of "Hamlet;"
yet I must add another, that I may ask you
a question about it. Do you agree with Falstaff that it is better to be on the wrong side
than on none, and do you think it a shame to
be on any but one?

The Squire. To a young man, like yourself,
I am always inclined to say Yes; to an old
one, No. The experience and observation of
years lead me to contract rather than enlarge
my sphere of possible knowledge. In politics,
even the statesman of genius rarely sees more
than his next step, and only after he has taken
that sees again the next. To me the pursuits
of the student of letters or the student of
science are far less interesting than those of
the young politician who aspires to the realization of his ideals of the constitution under
which he lives. As I said the other day, his
ideal seems to him complete and perfect, and
waiting only to be realized in actual life. It
is well that a man should begin his study of

life in the light of such an ideal, and that he
should believe that it is so true and good that
any contradiction must be wrong; and therefore I said, in answer to your former question,
that I should say to a young man it was wrong
to be on any side but one; that is, on the one
side which represents and embodies his own
ideal of the political life of his country. By
all means would I have him enjoy this his
honest belief; let him share heartily the triumphs of the party who hold up that ideal,
and in the fear that its loss will be the loss of
all that a good citizen holds dear. If these
things be absolutely true and right, then all
that opposes them must be false and wrong.
But if he has the wisdom and the courage to
look and see how his ideals stand the test of
experience, he will again and again see them
broken up and set aside by a force which they
are unable to resist, while the world not only
goes on just as before, but with such manifest
advantage that he is obliged, and eventually
glad, to confess that his ideal was not the
absolute law which governed the world of
politics, but only one small and partial representation of it. And so the old man answers
the other half of the question, and says that
it is *not* a shame to be on any side but one
in politics.

Foster. Then you do not think that there

is a right and a wrong side in party politics,
nor any such difference between Conservatives
and Liberals ?

The Squire. Not a pin to choose, so long as
the man honestly holds with either. There is
often much wrong-doing, much that is evil as
well as mistaken, in each party; but each
party represents one side, one half of the true
and the good, while it opposes the other. It
does not matter which leg you put into your
breeches first, said Dr. Johnson, but don't
stand there getting cold while you are doubt-
ing which leg it shall be.

Foster. Yet, Squire, I have heard you, at
our late meetings, stir the whole audience to
enthusiasm by telling them of the merits of
your side, and the wrong-doings of the other.

The Squire. That was counsel pleading for
client ; but the jury heard the other side, too,
before their verdict was given. Judgment followed, not for that constituency only, but for
the whole nation, through its representatives
in Parliament, and it will be found to be a
compromise, or " resolution of forces," with one
step forward on the line so indicated. Politics
mean action, not science nor even logic. New
things and new conditions of things are con-
stantly coming above the horizon, which had
never been dreamed of by our political philosophy. These demand action, not abstract

inquiry, and it is only in and by action that the right course is found. To act, you must take a side; you cannot be on both sides at once, though both have to be reckoned with in the end. The final action is really a joint one; not the triumph of a victor over the vanquished. If there were an absolute right and wrong in politics, it is inconceivable that the opinion of the whole nation should be — as we know it usually is — so nearly divided that the balance of parties is turned by a very small number of votes, and that this minority, though so little less than the majority, always acquiesces in the government of that majority. And so I say that Falstaff's doctrine, which you quote, is true if properly understood.

Foster. I should call this the philosophy of party. The practical view of Burke, that no political action can be effective unless men act together in a party, and to this end make mutual concessions and compromises among themselves, always seems to me intelligible and true, though one often hears it condemned by those who, as you say, sink below party while professing to rise above it. But when you speak so of the absence of an absolute right and wrong in politics, and of its being the business of a statesman merely to ascertain the next step, and to take that, may we not underrate the work really done by the great men who appear from time to time as the leaders of the nation? The British Constitution is often compared to an oak; may it not as properly be compared to a castle, or palace, or cathedral? May we not, in Ben Jonson's phrase, say that it is made as well as born, and that art gives the form and fashion to nature?

The Squire. Illustrations prove nothing, though they often throw light on a subject, and make an argument clearer by calling imagination to the aid of reason. Both your illustrations — the tree and the building — are good. Either will answer our purpose here. Let us take the oak. The oak has grown to be what it is in accordance with a law somehow contained in the original acorn. Its growth has somehow (we know not how) depended on the growth of its roots and branches; and while we cannot say that any one of these, however small, was not necessary to its growth, we may confidently say that it could not have become what it is without the vigorous growth of its greater roots and limbs. The whole is made up of its parts, and could never have existed without them; yet they have only come into existence, and still exist, as results of the original law in the acorn. And so it seems to me to be with the nation. It is not a mere metaphor to say that the life of a nation is a reality, a fact. This

national life is somehow made up of, or is one
with, the life of the men of the nation's successive generations. This life is more, not
less, strong and active in our great statesmen
than in our ordinary citizens. While we stand
close by some great personality of our own
generation, and watch his immediate action, it
seems as if his individual intellect and will
were directing and driving the course of events,
which he might have made otherwise if he had
so chosen ; but when an intervening distance
of time enables us to see what the whole course
of events has been, we discover that, great as
the man was, and great as was his mastery over
the events of the hour, he, no less than the
least important of the men around him, was
working in obedience to an irresistible law.
If you are not afraid of the language of Bacon
and Milton, you may say that this law is an
idea in the mind of God, which he has called
on his Englishmen to carry out in their national life. Anyhow, it is a law.

Foster. One question more. I have heard
you tell more than one meeting that the ballot
is secret beyond doubt ; but what do you say of
its morality ?

The Squire. I have often wished to deal with
that point while speaking, or in one of our leaflets, but, like Mr. Parker, have always been de-
terred by the fear I should make that "darker

which was dark enough without." The question is one of casuistry, a science, or an art, in which I have little skill.

Foster. Casuistry has, no doubt, a bad sound, like sophistry and jesuitism ; yet, if the case be really one of conscience, it must be possible as well as desirable to find some solution of it ; and so he must have thought who founded a professorship of casuistry and moral philosophy combined at Cambridge.

The Squire. Grote and John Mill had been all their lives in favor of the ballot ; but when it was at last carried they were found in the other camp. The intimidation of the shopkeepers by their customers in the great towns, for which the ballot had been demanded by the older Radicals, had almost died out ; and it was therefore surely better to retain the more manly form of open voting. And there are still politicians of the study rather than of the market-place, who insist on the loss of manliness in secret voting, and who overlook the facts obvious to all who remember the elections by open voting, and know that but for the ballot the voting must be carried on under the protection of soldiers as well as police, or there would be serious rioting.

Foster. Whatever the manliness of open voting under such protection, I admit that without it there could be only the traditional

manliness of Donnybrook Fair. But what of
the farm laborers and the village shopkeepers
in the counties? We have lately heard and
seen evidence enough of the great pressure,
call it legitimate or undue, put upon these
classes by the squires, the parsons, the farmers,
and even by their fellow-workmen. It is at
their peril if they do not promise their vote to
the candidate for whom it is demanded. Ought
they to keep that promise when given?

The Squire. I might put you off with some of
the old stories of the rustic humorists and
their evasions of the question how they had
voted : as when one said that when the friends
of the red candidate had solicited his vote he
had pleased them by his answer: he had no
less pleased the Primrose Dame by what he
promised her : and when he went to the poll
he pleased himself. Or when another told his
story thus : " When the blues asked for my
vote, I promised it to them ; then I promised
it to the reds when they canvassed me ; and
when I got into the polling-place by myself, I
said ' Conscience forever ! ' shut my eyes, and
made a cross somewhere on the paper, and
not even I know how I voted." But I am
afraid this will hardly answer your question.

Foster. Not quite. I think no one can
read the clauses of the Ballot Act without seeing that the act intends and provides not only

that it shall be unlawful for any man to try to
find out how another has voted, but also that
the voter shall be able to mislead and deceive
the man who does make the attempt.   But is
such deception moral as well as legal ?

The Squire.   If the voter's position is such
that he incurs only some social disfavor among
his neighbors if he does not deceive them as
to his vote, we should only pity his cowardice ;
but if he is a poor man, a laborer or a small
shopkeeper, who will really lose his work, or
the custom on which his livelihood depends, if
he is known to have voted against the will of
his employer or customer, the case is different.
Should he have no wife or child, he will no
doubt take the manlier and the better course if
he defies the intimidator and takes the consequence of refusing to say how he voted, though
I, at least, will not say that every man is to be
condemned who has not the courage to be a
martyr.   But if martyrdom is the nobler course
when the sacrifice is only of the man himself,
what if it includes his wife and children?   We
know the horrible story of the Scottish Cove-
nanter who was urged to recant by the torture,
not of himself, but of his child stretched on
the rack before his eyes.   I cannot think that
a man is called to endure such martyrdom as
that.   I say that *all* the guilt, not part of it,
lies on the head of the questioner ; and the

voter who is asked how he voted, and knows that the ruin of his wife and children hangs on his answer, not only has a moral right to deceive the man who asks the question, but ought to deceive him.

Foster. Even to telling a direct lie? I do not know why it is, but we always seem to make a distinction between a lie and an evasion, and to shrink from telling a lie, even while we think ourselves justified in resorting to an evasion which we mean to have the exact effect of the lie.

The Squire. It is an instinct, or a habit, which keeps us out of much mischief in ordinary life, though the Gospel seems to declare that the state of the heart is to be looked to, rather than the outward deed. And here the motive is good, though the act is not so. People who sit comfortably in their armchairs and condemn the wickedness of the poor man who tells his employer a lie as to the way he voted do not look at the whole case. The Constitution gives the man a vote, and it is his clear duty to use it, and that in accordance with his own judgment as to who is the right man to vote for. It is a plain question of conscience. He is bound to vote, and to vote according to his own belief as to the right side. If his wife and children are not to lose the daily bread which he earns for them, he

must promise his employer that he will vote
against his conscience. He makes the promise.
Is he bound to keep it or to break it? By the
wrongful act of his employer or customer, he
has been put in a position in which he must
do wrong either way; which course does his
conscience require him to take? On the one
hand, he must not only break his original
promise, but by any further lie which may be
needful conceal the fact that he has broken
it; on the other hand, he will have failed in
his duty to his country and his fellow-citizens
by voting for the man whom he believes not
to be the right one. It is a hard case of conscience. The man in the comfortable armchair
will most likely tell you that it is very easy.
To tell a lie, or series of lies, to an actual
employer is a plainly wicked act, though the
conduct of him who requires it cannot be de-
fended. But to be false to the duty you owe
your country is only to be false to a dim, far-
off abstraction; and it is surely pardonable to
do this as the lesser of the two evils? I cannot
think so. Luther preached against what the
reformers called the righteousness of the law,
warning the anxious seeker after that righteousness that he must beware that the devil
does not get possession of his conscience, and
so make him hear the devil's voice when he
thinks he is hearing that of God. It is a hard

case, not to be lightly settled by us who are not called to the responsibility of a decision for ourselves. Mrs. Gaskell, the most moral and most Christian of our novelists, has a tale which might be called "The Duty of Telling Lies." And I often think of that story of the Jacobite laird who was saved from the gallows by the false swearing of his old servant, who, when he was afterwards asked by his master how he, a God-fearing man, could have declared to such falsehoods in God's presence, replied, "I would rather trust my soul with the Lord than your body with the Whigs."

Foster. "Splendide mendax, et in omne virgo nobilis ævum."

The Squire. After all, our illustrations do not run on all fours with the thing illustrated. May it ever remain dishonest to an Englishman to tell a lie. But, "Woe to him through whom the offence cometh."

V.

LOVE AND MARRIAGE.

Hail, wedded Love!

MILTON.

THE sun was shining brightly and the church bells were pealing merrily, as we all walked back through the village from a wedding. The bride had been the playfellow, and then the maid, of the Squire's daughter; her father and mother lived in the village; and she had that morning been married to a young carpenter, with whom she was now to share a new home, not many miles away. I imagine that the Squire had given the young couple some substantial aid in setting up there; while his daughters had helped to make the new home bright for the future, as well as the old one gay for the wedding day. The Squire's daughter and eldest granddaughter had shared the office of bridesmaid with the bride's sister; but I learned with some surprise that there was to be no special merry-making at the Court, as the people in this part of the country call the manor house, while dropping the prefix of "Knighton," "Sutton," or whatever may be the name of the village in which the particular manor court was formerly held. After church we went with the wedding party to the cottage of the father and mother. There we all drank the health of the bride and bridegroom; the Squire spoke a few words of hope and of blessing, the ladies kissed the bride, and we walked homeward along the church path and up the avenue. I ventured to break the silence by asking the Squire's daughter how it was that her father, who had so many likings for the fine old English gentleman, all of the olden time, did not make the wedding of the daughter of people attached to his family by long services, an occasion for old-fashioned festivities of some kind.

"I am sure he is quite right," she replied. "At a wedding at which I was bridesmaid, not very long ago, the bride's father and mother insisted upon having what they called old-fashioned customs. So we had a long, dreary wedding breakfast, where the wretched bride sat opposite a huge cake, looking the picture of I don't know what, while the clergyman and her father and a number of other people made stupid speeches. Mr. Oldham, the bride's father, lamented that the good old wedding breakfasts, such as that at which we were, were going out of fashion, and that

people were now expected, on such occasions,
to swallow a biscuit and a cup of coffee, as if
they were at a railway station, with only five
minutes allowed. I thought the great tedious
breakfast horrid, and the new fashion much
better."

"But I dare say you had dancing in the
evening : and I am sure you like that."

"I do always delight in dancing," she returned. "Yet even that seemed out of place
on that evening ; it was so plain that the
mother and sisters were thinking of something
else than the company, and would have been
only too glad to have the house to themselves
in quiet. And I could not help feeling for
them, and losing all pleasure in the dancing.
But ask my father what he thinks about it all."

Here the young lady walked on "in maiden
meditation, fancy free," the rest of the party
dispersed, and I found myself alone with the
Squire at the top of the terrace steps. I said : —

"Your daughter has just been giving me
your reasons — or perhaps I should say her
own — for not having any merry-making up
here after the wedding."

The Squire. That is a kind of paternal government or paternal patronage for which I have
no liking. The children are grown up and
have homes of their own ; and we must respect
those homes, however humble. There are

happy as well as sad times for thoughts and feelings which can be shared only by the two or three nearest to us. Such sympathy as it was possible for us to show to-day we have shown by going to church, and there taking our place in the one great family: to attempt more seems to me a sort of intrusion, and even profanation. We know little, and share less, of the deeper thoughts and feelings of those nearest to us : how can we know or share those of these poor people, divided from us by lines of impassable reserve and reticence ? This morning, while I thought of other marriages, past and to come, and of Tennyson's pictures of the bride when first she wears the orange flower and when she returns to her old home again, I considered, too, how certainly these good people were happy in the like thoughts and feelings, though they had never read Tennyson, nor put these thoughts and feelings into words like his. Depend upon it, there is as much and as true romance in the young hearts, and in the old ones, too, in that cottage as in those in this house.

Foster. You say the romance of old hearts, too : then may I believe that you do not think love a mere fading flower, which must soon perish ? If you had long ago written such a poem as Coleridge's " Love," you would not have prefixed to it, any number of years after-wards, those verses of Petrarch ?

The Squire. I know the poem well. It is full
of that soft beauty of images, emotion, and expression with which Coleridge so often reminds
us of Shakespeare and Spenser. But what of
Petrarch's verses ?

Foster. After the customary classical phrases
about the wounds inflicted by Cupid's arrows,
he says that age has changed all this ; and that
when he reads his youthful verses again *mens
horret*, he shrinks from the voice and words
which sound like those of another, and not his
own. I am glad you do not agree with Coleridge in this cynical mocking at his own belief.

The Squire. There is another poem of Coleridge's, a charming piece of prose and verse,
called "The Improvisatore," in which he himself replies to and puts aside that cynical doctrine which you regret. Coleridge's ideas of
love, and of life generally, are always high and
noble, — no man's higher ; but in their realization he fell far short. He had the intellect of
a wise man and the conscience of a good man,
but a will weak and unstable in the extreme ;
and great teacher as he was to his generation,
and will be to generations yet to come, there
was but too much reason for the remorse with
which he mourned, but could not in this life
redeem, his own shortcomings. He was no
doubt sincere when he said, —

" To be beloved is all I need,
And whom I love, I love indeed ; "

but side by side with this is the fact that he
could not live with his wife and the mother of his
children. We have all more or less reason to
know with remorse what it is to be possessed
of the evil spirit of contradiction ; but the worst
form of this possession is that which separates
husband and wife from heart and hearth. You
cannot wonder that poor Coleridge one day
made the cynical lines of Petrarch his own, and
another the words of belief in an undying love
in which Beaumont and Fletcher, Burns and
Moore, have embodied that faith. In one
sense it is true that love is a fading flower ; but
it is still more true that just as the promises of
childhood and youth find their fulfillment in
mature age, so the aspirations and hopes of
youthful lovers find their fulfillment in the
after years of marriage. It is only in a continually expanding and maturing union of husband and wife that the realization is possible
of such a love as Charles pictures to Angelina
when he says : —

" We 'll live together, like two neighbor vines,
Circling our souls and loves in one another !
We 'll spring together, and we 'll bear one fruit ;
One joy shall make us smile, and one grief mourn ;
One age go with us, and one hour of death
Shall close our eyes, and one grave make us happy."

Foster. I am glad to hear you say so. But

how long the world has taken to accept this
faith; how imperfectly does it now practice it,
or even believe it! Christ told his disciples that
it would be found in the story of the creation
of man: it glimmers in the love of Jacob for
Rachel: the favorite allegory of the Hebrew
prophets of their nation as the bride of Jehovah seeming to show that the ideal had some
counterpart in actual life.   Homer shows us
the love of husband and wife in Hector and
Andromache; but in the days of Plato all recognition of a relation between love and marriage seems utterly to have vanished.

The Squire. Yes; and how slowly and with
what struggles has it been emerging through
the ages of the new Christian civilization!
Socrates, or Plato for him, dreamed, as you
say, of a purely ideal love, with no relation to
actual life.   The Christian Church tried long
and earnestly to purify and carry into a spiritual channel the passion of love, by making
Christ or the Virgin Mary, St. Joseph or St.
Catherine, or some other of the holy men and
women who had been raised to sainthood, the
objects of the passionate devotions of monks
and nuns.   I respect and admire the self-
sacrifice and the devotion with which these
monks and nuns gave themselves up to this
spiritual love; and I cannot doubt that they
were helping to lay the foundations for a life

more really spiritual, because more in accordance with God's laws of human nature than
their own. To some, indeed, it was given to
realize their ideas of spiritual love. But they
were, and still are, the exceptions.

Foster. Do you think, then, that the poetic
ideal of love, such as we have it in the lines you
have just quoted from Beaumont and Fletcher,
or as it stands in " John Anderson, my Jo," is in
truth identical with the ideal of the Christian
Church ?

The Squire. I often think that in the marriage
service which we have heard this morning,
and especially in the marriage vows, our English Church reformers have embodied the very
ideals of love, in itself, and in the married life.
The words are homely enough, but there is a
pathos, a depth of feeling in them, which cannot be greater. " I. Richard, take thee, Mary,
to my wedded wife, to have and to hold
from this day forward, for better for worse, for
richer or poorer, in sickness and in health, to
love and to cherish, till death us do part, according to God's holy ordinance ; and thereto
I plight thee my troth." If love be the giving
one's self without reserve to another, and receiving the like gift from that other, what words
could express such love better than these ?

Foster. Not even those of Sir Philip Sidney : —

" My true-love hath my heart, and I have his,
 By just exchange for one another given :
 I hold his dear, and mine he cannot miss,
 There never was a better bargain driven :
 My true love hath my heart, and I have his.

" His heart in me keeps him and me in one,
 My heart in him his thoughts and senses guides :
 He loves my heart, for once it was his own,
 I cherish his because in me it bides :
 My true-love hath my heart, and I have his."

The Squire. It is of the essence of love, that longing desire to share the joys and the troubles of life with the loved one, and the confident belief that we can so share the burdens and double the enjoyments of him or her whom we love ; and what words can say this better than " for better for worse, for richer for poorer, in sickness and in health "? " To love and to cherish " in all those chances and changes, — the most ardent, most romantic lover cannot promise more ; and happy is that man or woman who, at the end of a long married life, can say, though with many tender and even sad regrets, " I have kept my vows "!

Foster. Is it not said that in the old York Manual, in use before the Reformation, along with the vows as they now stand were the words " for fairer for fouler "?

The Squire. So Wheatley says. It is just what Moore says in the song beginning, —

 " Believe me, if all those endearing young charms,
 Which I gaze on so fondly to-day."

The meaning is good in the quaint old phrase; but it is not every one who can hear grave thoughts expressed in words of humorous oddity without an incongruous sense of the ridiculous, and therefore our reformers were right to omit them.

Foster. There are two vows or promises which you have not noticed: the woman's vow to obey, and the man's declaration "with my body I thee worship."

The Squire. They are the counterparts of one sentiment, that which we call the sentiment of chivalry. You always recognize that sentiment with prompt alacrity. The spontaneous and heartfelt reverence for woman, which we call chivalry is not given to all men, not even to all good men; nor do all women seem to feel the need for it strongly, though no doubt all are pleased when such worship is shown them. I suppose it can never be wholly wanting in the love of the young; but with some men it seems transient, and sometimes it degenerates into a foolish gallantry, or, still worse, into that detestable combination of outward respect and inward contempt which Lord Chesterfield held to be the proper attitude of a gentleman. But I know that you are, and will be till death, a true knight among ladies. Then as to the counterpart in the woman's vow of obedience. There are many forms and many degrees of that obedience; and every woman must judge, and every good woman will judge rightly, what these must be in her own case. You may study them all in Shakespeare, in every variety; no two alike, but all very beautiful. I will give you one, that of Portia, in "The Merchant of Venice,"— Portia, the rich heiress, mistress of herself and her wealth, self-possessed and self-asserting, whom we may suspect of being half conscious of her own intellectual superiority to the worthy and amiable man whom she has chosen to take for her husband, and of whom she makes fun with saucy boldness, while she is getting him and his friend out of a difficulty beyond their wit to cope with. This is how Portia gives herself to Bassanio : —

> " You see me, Lord Bassanio, where I stand,
>   Such as I am : though for myself alone
>   I would not be ambitious in my wish,
>   To wish myself much better ; yet, for you
>   I would be trebled twenty times myself ;
>   A thousand times more fair, ten thousand times
>   More rich ;
>   That only to stand high in your account,
>   I might in virtues, beauties, livings, friends,
>   Exceed account ; but the full sum of me
>   Is sum of something, which, to term in gross,
>   Is an unlesson'd girl, unschool'd, unpractised,
>   Happy in this, she is not yet so old
>   But she may learn ; happier than this,
>   She is not bred so dull but she can learn ;
>   Happiest of all is that her gentle spirit

Commits itself to yours to be directed,
As from her lord, her governor, her king.
Myself and what is mine to you and yours
Is now converted: but now I was the lord
Of this fair mansion, master of my servants,
Queen o'er myself; and even now, but now,
This house, these servants and this same myself
Are yours, my lord: I give them with this ring;
Which when you part from, lose, or give away,
Let it presage the ruin of your love
And be my vantage to exclaim on you."

The whole scene is, indeed, a perfect picture of true love, — love at once passionate and pure, as modest and as chaste as it is without reserve.

Foster. Portia's words which you have repeated remind me of the words with which the young Roman matron crossed the threshold of her husband's house and her future home, — "Ubi tu Caius, ego Caia."

The Squire. Which Wheatley well translates, "Where you are master, I am mistress." There is a proud humility in the words which well becomes the dignity of the Roman matron. And no words could better sum up and describe that most charming among the things of daily life, the wife's unconscious faith and assertion that the home which she shares with her husband is as much and as really her own by right of marriage as it is his by inheritance or by the work of his own hands. It is this twofold life, two beings and two lives in one, which makes a marriage and a home.

Foster. You remind me of the description of the Dauphin and the Lady Blanch in "King John : " —

> " If lusty love should go in quest of beauty,
>   Where should he find it fairer than in Blanch?
>   If zealous love should go in search of virtue,
>   Where should he find it purer than in Blanch?
>   If love ambitious sought a match of birth,
>   Whose veins bound richer blood than Lady Blanch?
>   Such as she is, in beauty, virtue, birth,
>   Is the young Dauphin every way complete :
>   If not complete of, say he is not she ;
>   And she again wants nothing, to name want,
>   If want it be not that she is not he :
>   He is the half part of a blessed man,
>   Left to be finished by such as she ;
>   And she a fair divided excellence,
>   Whose fulness of perfection lies in him."

I should be glad enough to believe heartily in the lastingness of all true love, whether on the authority of Shakespeare or any other. But does not Shakespeare mean Prospero to confess that even the holy love of Ferdinand and Miranda is but such stuff as dreams are made of ?

The Squire. He charges himself with the petulance of old age while he so speaks. If he had really believed this, could he have said, when he saw how love was awaking in those young hearts, —

> " So glad of this as they I cannot be,
>   Who are surprised withal : but my rejoicing
>   At nothing can be more " ?

He could not have rejoiced to lose his
daughter, that most dear companion of his
old age, for the sake of a dream. I do not
pretend that all love, even when it has the
signs of being true, is always lasting. It is
too often choked, and perishes under the
pleasures or the cares of the world. Yet,
depend upon it, as you grow older you will see
more and more instances and proofs of the
reality and the depth of the love of husbands
and wives for each other in the most ordinary,
commonplace couples. I have heard of marriages where love has died out from some
canker of selfishness or worldliness at its
heart; but I have oftener seen unexpected
proofs of a love stronger than death in all
sorts of people in whom I had never before
discovered any signs of sentiment or romance.
Nor must we forget the many loving couples
in whose case love has come after a marriage
which seemed to have had no higher than
prudential motives of one kind or another.
Love, indeed, must be kept alive by love, —
love deep in the heart, yet coursing through
the minutest veins, and giving to every power
of life a new and double power. Love must
show itself living in the great occasions of life,
in some supreme moment calling for mutual
sympathy in a great joy or grief; it must show
itself in all the thousand little daily and hourly

thoughtfulnesses, courtesies, and forbearances
of common life. These things, the reflection
of which we call good manners, the manners of
the lady and the gentleman, should have with
husband and wife a reality as of sunlight
compared with moonlight. They alone can
know and share these things in their fullness,
and they should be to them as the atmosphere
they breathe. And it is noticeable that in the
old Marriage Service the bride's vow of obedience included a promise to be "buxom at
bed and board," where the earlier sense of the
word "buxom" as "obedient" is evidently
meant to include the later one of good-hu-
mored, genial obedience, as when Milton joins
it with "blithe and debonair." I think the
author of "Obiter Dicta" says that husband
and wife should take care to have and to keep
up a common interest in some subject of
reading or action which they can always share
together. It is good practical advice. To
many it may be unnecessary, and especially
to those who have children as the objects of
their common love and care. I once heard a
noble-minded lady say sadly, "We were very
much in love with each other," speaking of
the old days of courtship; and she added,
"and it might all come back again if only he
would show me some love." They were not
selfish nor ungenerous, but their life was cold

and dreary because they had not learned
rightly the arts of wedded love. A wise and
prudent reserve in all other affairs of life is
so right and needful that there is always
danger of its growing up in the one relation
in which there should be no reserve ; and so
it may grow and harden till it becomes an
impassable barrier between the hearts that
should be one. When Maurice was asked
whether we shall know one another in the life
to come, he answered, in his favorite Socratic
fashion, with the further question, "Do we
know one another here?" There is a strange
perverseness of our nature by which we recoil
from sympathy with ourselves at the very
moment at which we are craving for that
sympathy, and when to love and to be loved
is the very thing we are longing for. I am
thinking not of the great occasions and duties
of married life, but of its little daily and
hourly courtesies and endearments. They tell
us that the great oak draws its nourishment
and life not more through its main roots than
through its countless minute fibres and threads
which feed those main roots below and its
countless leaves above. "To love and to
cherish," — it is this sympathy in giving and
receiving of souls that we cherish as well as
love the object of our vows. When you marry,
as I hope you will, do not forget the advice of
an old man.

Foster. You ought to know what you say; and I, as I said just now, am only too willing to believe it. Yet those awful words which we heard this morning haunt me, — "Till death us do part!"

The Squire. They are indeed awful; as he knows best who has heard them at the grave-side echoed back in the words of another church service, — " Earth to earth, ashes to ashes, dust to dust." Cicero's Cato declares that he would not think life worth living if he did not believe that he should meet his lost son again among all the company of heaven, as his words might almost literally be translated. And if this was the faith of a heathen philosopher, much more may it be ours. If one grave is to make the lovers happy, — and Beaumont and Fletcher express a deeply rooted thought and sentiment in many hearts, — it must be because they look beyond that grave. The ballad of John Anderson is perfect in its kind, but I always like to think of it along with its supplement in Lady Nairne's "Land o' the Leal." To sleep together at the foot of the hill which the old loving hearts had climbed together long years before is a pleasant thought, yet surely pleasant only to those who look to share the fast-coming joy of a waking from that sleep to be shared together in that better land.

" For if this earth be ruled by Perfect Love,
   Then, after his brief range of blameless days,
   The toll of funeral in an Angel ear
   Sounds happier than the merriest marriage-bell.
   The face of Death is toward the Sun of Life,
   His shadow darkens earth : his truer name
   Is 'Onward,' no discordance in the roll
   And march of that Eternal Harmony
   Whereto the worlds beat time, tho' faintly heard
   Until the great Hereafter. Mourn in hope !"

We had come into the house as the Squire repeated these lines half to himself. Then, going into his own room, he took from a drawer a book, which he opened, and pointed to the following words : —

" When I think how these hands cared for me in sickness and in health, I feel that I shall press them to my heart again ; when I see, in memory, those lips which ever spoke in words of wisdom and comfort and tenderest love and trust, and those bright joyous eyes which to the last bended their light on me, I know that I shall most certainly behold that face and hear that voice again, — in the resurrection. It cannot be otherwise. The expression of such spirits, which is indeed their lifelong character stamping itself upon the outward form, can never die. 'There is a natural body, and there is a spiritual body,' says St. Paul."

The Squire sat down in his armchair ; and we were silent for some time. Then I said, —

"They are beautiful words: where do they come from?"

The Squire. They are slightly altered from Miss Bremer's "Homes of the New World." They express the thought, or rather let me say the conviction and the faith, summed up by Tennyson in the words, "We shall know them when we meet."

Foster. Has not Tennyson opened a new road in literature, in what he writes so freely as to another life, or rather as to our life after death?

The Squire. I think this is so, if in your use of the word Literature you draw a line which shall put on one side Shakespeare, and on the other the New Testament, the Pilgrim's Progress, and all our Hymns of the Christian Church.

Foster. That is what I meant; but I see the great difficulty of doing anything of the kind. You may ask me whether I do not consider the writings of our great theologians to be a part of English literature, and I should hardly know what to answer.

The Squire. No; so far from wishing to push you into a corner, I think you are right. There is a real distinction, though it should be one of relationship, not of separation between our thoughts of this life and of that which is to come. Poets and men of letters deal principally with the one, and preachers and theologians with the other; but Tennyson, while belonging to the former, has put himself in touch with the latter, with more openness and less of reticence than usual. Wordsworth was a sincere and devout Christian, but there is a striking difference between his great "Ode" and Tennyson's "In Memoriam." The Idea, the Motive, underlying Wordsworth's Ode is that Man has in him another and truer life than that of Nature, of which he has indications in himself which seem like the recollections of a divine Mind whence he has come; while in Tennyson's poem the Master thought is going forward into a world to come. Conversely, it has been said of Maurice, the greatest of the religious teachers of our generation, that he dwells so naturally on the present reality of the life eternal that he sometimes seems to speak little of the future life everlasting. But the ideas are really interchangeable, and he knows most of the one, to whom the other is best known, whichever he may find it his own vocation to speak upon.

Foster. But there are good and thoughtful men who heartily recognize the reality of a moral life above that of mere nature, and yet have no belief, but indeed a positive disbelief, of any continuance of this life beyond the grave?

The Squire. As I often say to you, the world is full of mysteries which I cannot fathom. I have asked myself your question many times; the only answer I find is that in the Gospel: "And His disciples asked Him, saying, Master, who did sin, this man, or his parents, that he was born blind? Jesus answered, Neither hath this man sinned nor his parents: but that the works of God should be made manifest in him." He may have found his new experience worth the price of the old one when the Divine Word said, "Let there be light and there was light."

Foster. Why does Shakespeare, who knew everything, say almost nothing about a future life? Shakespeare's ghosts, like all the ghosts of actual life, are but the projected forms of the imagination of him who sees them, and tell nothing which he did not know already. "To sleep, perchance to dream," and to dream very uneasily, is all that Hamlet's philosophy can tell him of another life. And Constance can think of it only as a place where her child will not know her, but will be lost to her forever.

The Squire. Shakespeare's business was to picture men and women as they are, in themselves, and in their relations to each other. Shakespeare's men and women are not religious people, but they are the men and women of actual life. Like the greater part of actual men and women, they are not god- less, nor unbelieving either in the force of prayer or in the reality of a future life; but they are mainly occupied with the affairs of this world, and its duties and its ambitions, its griefs and its enjoyments; and their chief thought of death is that it is the rest from all these labors.

Foster.

> " Fear no more the heat o' the sun,
> Nor the furious winter's rages;
> Thou thy worldly task hast done,
> Home art gone and ta'en thy wages ;"

and

> " Good-night, sweet prince,
> And flights of angels sing thee to thy rest."

The Squire. Yes. But notice the words are those of one who never uses a word that is not the exact counterpart of the thought it expresses. In the passage you quote from Cymbeline, not only has the whole manifest reference to the Scripture words, " Blessed are the dead that die in the Lord henceforth, for they rest from their labours, and their works do follow them," but each word is sig- nificant of another life. A divine taskmaster, of tasks other than of this world, a home in which shall be enjoyed the reward for work here done well — all these are plainly implied.

Then, again, look at Horatio's farewell to
Hamlet. The true commentary on that "Good-
night" is Mrs. Barbauld's "Hymn of Life,"
of which Wordsworth said to a lady from
whom the story comes down to me, that to
have written that poem he would willingly
have left half his own unwritten. You can
repeat it — turning to his daughter who had
joined us ; to which she answered : —

> "Life! I know not what thou art,
>   But know that thou and I must part;
>   And when, or how, or where we met,
>   I own, to me's a secret yet.
>   Life! we've been long together,
>   Through pleasant and through cloudy weather;
>   'T is hard to part when friends are dear —
>   Perhaps 't will cost a sigh, a tear;
>   — Then steal away, give little warning,
>   Choose thine own time;
>   Say not Good-night — but in some brighter clime
>   Bid me Good-morning."

The Squire. Yes; "good-night" tells certainly of "good-morning," with all the bright
and glad thoughts which belong to the beginning of a new day. "Rest," too, does not less
certainly imply renewal of life and strength
to new work, because it has come to one
weary from past overwork. And even in the
interval of rest Hamlet is accompanied by the
songs of angels. And among them we may
be certain was Ophelia. She had become a
"ministering angel," as Laertes was assured,

and that she was still his sister, while he laid " her fair and unpolluted flesh " in the grave.

Foster. But does Shakespeare mean all this?

The Squire. He says it all; I do not pretend to know more than that. As I said just now, his men and women are not religious people ; he has no St. Francis nor Saint Teresa, no Thomas à Kempis, nor Madame Guion ; but he shows us real men and women, who think, feel, and act as real men and women for the most part do.

Foster. You mean that only a few in any generation are called and have power given to them, consciously to look on the present life as the preparation for that which is to come.

The Squire. Yes; it is only in that way that I meant to speak of men and women as possibly not religious. It is not till the shades of Saturday night are falling that the thoughts of home and wages take the place of those of work and duty, even in good men and women. It is only in this sense that I would dare to say that men are not religious, and even so I do not pretend to know men's hearts, nor to doubt that in many a heart and mind lie thoughts and feelings too deep for words. I call a man religious who lives in habitual consciousness of his relation to God ; but the relationship itself is in fact infinitely deeper than the consciousness of it.

Foster.

> " Dear child! dear girl! that walkest with me here,
>   If thou appear untouch'd by solemn thought
>   Thy nature is not therefore less divine;

> " Thou liest in Abraham's bosom all the year,
>   And worship'st at the Temple's inner shrine,
>   God being with thee when we know it not."

The Squire. Yes ; or take, for instance, that
speech of Portia which I quoted just now, in
which there is not a word which can in this
sense be called religious, and yet it implies
throughout the Christian ideal of marriage as
a divinely created and sanctioned bond. And
so I think Shakespeare may be justified as
true to nature, even to those who have the
heartiest sympathy with Tennyson's " In Memoriam."

Foster. From what you have said of Shakespeare, I seem to get some light on a question
that has always been a great puzzle to me, as
I suppose it has been to many others both
before and since Bishop Warburton : Why
there is so little said by the writers of the Old
Testament about a future life, although the
subject must have been familiar to them in the
form in which it was treated by their neighbors, the Egyptians. History shows us that
the Eschatology — is not that the word ? —
of the Egyptians was not so favorable to the
moral and intellectual growth and vigor of

national life, as was the simpler and almost negative faith of the Hebrews. Though there are passages in the Psalms of a more cheerful kind, the words of the pious Hezekiah as to the unknown world of the dead are at least as gloomy as those of the heroes of Homer and Virgil.

The Squire. The Jews seem to have felt the uncertainties as to a future life no less than did the Greeks and Romans, who rose to such hopes as those of Plato and Cicero, or sank to the blank nothingness of Moschus or of Horace. It was that preaching of the Resurrection which the Athenians thought the words of a babbler, which shifted the centre and pivot of man's life, and so gave birth to the Christian faith in a life eternal.

Foster. And I suppose you will say that the change caused by the new faith is reflected in the popular imagination by the change from the descent into Pluto's gloomy realm across the Styx by help of Charon and his boat, to the crossing of the Jordan at the summons of the messengers whose raiment shone like gold and their faces as the light, and the going up to the Celestial City and into the presence of its King with chariots and horses and triumphal music, by Bunyan's pilgrims.

The Squire. Yes. And I like to think that it was Bunyan's latest experience which led him to describe Christiana's passage of the River as one in which there was nothing but joy, without even that small measure of fear which Christian had for a moment felt, as the waters went over his head. I often think that that description of the arrival of the Messenger, and of Christiana's glad obedience to his summons, is what I should wish to hear read to me in the hour when my own summons has come.

But hark! the bells have begun again. The friendly ringers who welcomed the bride and bridegroom to church in the morning are now speeding them on their going away. And this talk of ours, serious as it has become, is, I hope, not unfittingly rounded with the joyful and merry peal.

VI.

BOOKS : TENNYSON AND MAURICE.

Wondrous indeed is the virtue of a true Book.
                                        CARLYLE.

                The man that is dear to God.
                        TENNYSON TO MAURICE.

IT was raining hard ; and as it is the fashion, in a country house, to like a fire on a wet day even in summer, we sat before the logs blazing on the hearth in the Great Parlor, while in front of us sat purring the family cat, who answered, when he thought fit to answer, to the name of Jim. Books were all round us, and our talk naturally turned on them. I said, —

"Of all our English books existing and to come, how many will always live ?"

The Squire. There are two ways in which a book may live. It may live, age after age, in itself, like one of our great oaks, as Carlyle has finely described it in "Sartor Resartus." I think the book is on the table : pray read the passage.

Foster (takes the book, turns over the pages, and reads). " Wondrous, indeed, is the virtue

of a true Book. Not like a dead city of
stones, yearly crumbling, yearly needing re-
pair; more like a tilled field, but then a
spiritual field: like a spiritual tree, let me
rather say, it stands from year to year, and
from age to age (we have Books that already
number some hundred and fifty human ages);
and yearly comes its new produce of leaves
(Commentaries, Deductions, Philosophical, Political Systems; or were it only Sermons, Pam-
phlets, Journalistic Essays), every one of which
is talismanic and thaumaturgic, for it can per-
suade men. O thou who art able to write a
Book, which once in the two centuries or
oftener there is a man gifted to do, envy not
him whom they name City-builder, and inex-
pressibly pity him whom they name Conqueror
or City-burner! Thou too art a Conqueror
and Victor, but of the true sort, namely, over
the Devil; thou too hast built what will outlast
all marble and metal, and be a wonder-bringing
city of the mind, a Temple and Seminary and
Prophetic Mount, whereto all kindreds of the
Earth will pilgrim. Fool! why journeyest thou
wearisomely in thy antiquarian fervor to gaze
on the stone pyramids of Geeza or the clay
ones of Sacchara? These stand there, as I
can tell thee, idle and inert, looking over the
Desert, foolishly enough, for the last three
thousand years; but canst thou not open thy

Hebrew Bible, thus, or even Luther's version thereof ? "

The Squire. For " Luther's " read " the English " and then add Shakespeare, and you will have one answer to your question. I cannot doubt that so long as English shall endure as the speech of a civilized people, so long will the English Bible and Shakespeare endure; and English-speaking people will still, like Archbishop Sharp, owe all their success in life to those two books.

Foster. Did Archbishop Sharp know anything of either the English Bible or Shakespeare ?

The Squire. Not the Archbishop of tragic Scottish history, but the Archbishop of York, Queen Anne's trusted counselor, who, Burnet tells us, so spoke of what he owed to the Bible and Shakespeare, and used to recommend the like studies to the young clergy. And Tennyson is said to have advised a young man to read a verse of the Bible and one of Shakespeare every day. " From the one," he said, " you will learn your relations with God ; from the other, your relations with man." But there is another way in which books live. To illustrate this, let me go from Carlyle to Chaucer :

> " Out of the olde fieldes, as men saith
> Cometh all this new corn, from year to year.
> And out of olde bookes, in good faith,
> Cometh all this new science that men lere."

Without working the illustration to death, we
may say that, with a very few exceptions, the
knowledge which we derive from books is not
derived direct from the original books in which
it was first brought forth, but from a succession of new books, in which the experiences
and the thoughts of the preceding generation
are represented with the new developments
and in the new forms suited to the new generation. Each year yields its harvest of new
books, which supply our mental and moral
food for the day, and no more; while a small
portion of the knowledge they contain becomes a reserve of seed corn, which is resown
to provide the new books of the next year or
the next generation. If we say, with Chaucer,
that the new knowledge comes from the old
books, as the new wheat does from the old
fields, we must then shift the comparison, and
say that the new books are the new corn, and
that the old books have lost their individuality,
ceasing to be more than the clods of the
ploughed fields.

Foster. I believe you might have quoted
Carlyle as well as Chaucer for this comparison,
too. I think he somewhere says, perhaps quoting Goethe, "A loaf of bread is good and
satisfying for a single day; but corn cannot
be eaten, and seed corn must not be ground."
But do you think that the Bible and Shake-

speare are the only books which will themselves live on so long as the world of civilization lasts?   Even within the limits of English-
speaking civilization, will not Paradise Lost
and The Pilgrim's Progress live on, not
merely in spirit, but in their actual old forms?

The Squire. Since the art of printing has
come in aid of the earlier institution of public
libraries, it may seem impossible that anything short of an universal return to barbarism
should utterly destroy the great masterpieces
of literature, ancient or modern, so that they
should no longer live in the very forms in
which they were first given to the world.   Yet
we know that the readers of each of such
books are a small and limited class ; and of
these, again, the number is still smaller of
readers who find in the particular book the
last and the best expression of the subject of
which it treats.   Poetry must always be read
for its own sake, and there will always be a
few who will continue thus to read Homer
and Horace, Dante, Chaucer and Spenser, for
their own sake.   But even of those who in
each generation are really lovers of poetry, by
far the greater number will seek and find what
they want in the poets of their own time,
because such poets most directly bring forth
the deepest thoughts and feelings of that time ;
while the reader of the older poetry must be

able — and every one is not able — either to translate old thoughts into new for himself, or else to transport himself in imagination into the far-off time and place to which the book before him belongs. And when we turn from poetry to philosophy, history, or science, it is mainly, if not entirely, for the sake of the materials which the old books supply for making new ones that the old are studied. In each of these kinds of knowledge there is an absolute need that the old facts, arguments, and methods of thought and reasoning should be reproduced in new forms, generation after generation. To do this work, through the study of the old books, is the calling of one or two men in each generation ; and they, and they only, find in themselves the ability for the work. Such a student will no doubt often be charmed by the style and language of the book itself, be it Plato, Aristotle, Cicero, Bacon, Tacitus, Hume, or Gibbon ; but his main business will still be with the materials which his author supplies for new work.

Foster. I cannot deny that there is a good deal of truth in what you say; but I am glad to believe that, like a man who belongs to several London clubs, I belong to several of those limited classes of readers of old books, and that there are a good many books beside the Bible and Shakespeare which I can read and enjoy for their own sakes. But may I ask you again whether you think those the only two books of universal interest to English-speaking men, at least? Will you not include Paradise Lost and the Pilgrim's Progress with these, and indeed some others, too, which I could name?

The Squire. I decline to dogmatize. I am too old to believe that I possess any formula which will methodize and explain the facts of the universe. I feel more certain about the Bible and Shakespeare than about any other books; but there are others, and especially those you mention, as to which facts are at present in favor of their personal immortality, if I may use so vile a phrase. The religious and the human interest of Paradise Lost and The Pilgrim's Progress are of the highest, and you may almost say that every one who reads at all reads both of these books. Every one to whom the conflict of nature and spirit is a practical reality, and many to whom it is only a curiously interesting dream, find the most lifelike representation of this conflict in Bunyan's allegory. And Milton embodies for us in forms at once of deepest human interest and perfect beauty of imagination, thought, and language, the most popular and most widely accepted attempt to solve the great problem of the existence of evil, and so

lighten the burden and the mystery which
have weighed so heavily on us in all ages.

Foster. That is indeed the awful riddle of
the Sphinx, which she calls on every thoughtful man to answer, or be devoured. Happy is
he who can even baffle or otherwise put off
the question which no one can answer! You
cannot think that Milton has done more than
this? He invokes the highest inspiration, that
he may rise to the height of this great argument, and justify the ways of God to man;
but in truth he gets no further than St. Paul
had done before him when he declared that
those ways were past finding out. Indeed,
Milton seems, half cynically, to admit this to
be so, when, later on, he makes the more
amiable of his devils sit on a hill retired,
discussing these questions till they lose themselves in wandering mazes. The answer that
came to Job out of the whirlwind was only
that finite and mortal man cannot fathom the
purposes and the methods of the Almighty
Creator of the universe; nor does the writer
of the book, in his visionary narrative, carry
the argument any further. The book of Eccle-
siastes, that practical summary of the worldly
experiences of man's frustrated ideals and
hopes of life, can give no other conclusion of
the matter than the direction to "fear God
and keep his commandments; for this is the

whole duty of man." Nor does St. Paul help us. He declares, indeed, with entire confidence and conviction, that the problem will hereafter be solved in the complete and absolute triumph of good over evil ; but after an attempt to apply his argument to the story of Pharaoh, in a way which I must think no argument at all, he gives it up, and falls back, as I said just now, on that which still remains the only answer. I forget how Robinson Crusoe evaded the difficulty when Friday asked him, in the course of his religious education, "Why God no kill devil?" I suppose, by making a metaphysical distinction between necessity and free will. Our modern Agnostics, interested only in physical science, will say that they do not know whether there be any God or devil, and so pass by on the other side. There is no answer to the Sphinx's riddle ; but to say that there is no riddle is to deny half the facts of our life.

The Squire. I quite agree with you. Indeed, you have understated your case and its complications. Not only is the existence of evil a mystery to all who believe intelligently in a wise and good Creator, but there is the yet deeper mystery that all the higher forms of any human virtue, affection, sympathy, are called forth by the contradiction of corresponding forms of evil ; nay, the highest of

all, self-sacrifice for the sake of others, seems
to owe its very existence to the evil which it
rises up to meet. A man may judge for himself whether the sufferings of mind or body
which he is called on to endure are compensated, or more than compensated, by the blessings which they have brought with them, and
giving, as they so often do, a double power to
every power above their original functions and
offices. But how can it be morally worth
while that the highest goodness and happiness
of some men should have as necessary conditions not merely the suffering and misery of
others, but even their crimes and sins? And
again, how can it be reasonable or right that
my happiness, however great, should have been
bought by the horrible sufferings of the mar-
tyrs by whom it has been so won? You may
say that they were willing to pay that price for
the happiness of a world. I believe they were
so willing; but how can I have any moral right
to benefit by a sacrifice such as I certainly
could not make myself? I have no doubt —
I am heartily convinced — that there is a solution to the problem, an answer to the Sphinx;
and I could supply myself with more than one
fanciful explanation which I like better than
those of my neighbors. But I do not pretend
to understand, nor that any understanding is
possible for me till I have crossed the bar.

Foster. You quote Tennyson : do you think he has given us any new light on the subject ? It has manifestly occupied his deepest thoughts and feelings, and influenced his whole career as a poet.

The Squire. I think he is the greatest teacher of our generation in this matter. He has stated the question in the most complete and adequate way in which it is possible to state it, — for our generation, at least ; for each age has it own way of looking at such questions, and demands its own requirements to be respected. His " In Memoriam " sets out fully, and his poem of " Vastness " and that on the death of the Duke of Clarence sum up in the plainest terms, the real problem, without any shirking or evasion. With equal clearness he points out the direction to which he must look for the solution which will come hereafter ; and he declares, and calls on all true hearts to accept, his conviction that the death of those we love is the link which connects the now insoluble problem with the promise that it shall be one day answered.

Foster. Yes ; Tennyson states the insoluble problem without reticence or rhetorical evasion. He talks no stuff about partial evil being universal good, or of good and evil being opposite sides of a whole, in which they are equally necessary complements of each other.

He treats them as not merely opposites, but as
contradictory. There is no place for evil in
his ideal of a perfect universe. There can be
no belief in a divine Creator, and no peace or
happiness for the heart of man, but in the
ultimate elimination and destruction of all evil,
moral and physical. But does he carry us any
farther than this?

The Squire. One step, at least ; and I should
say more than one. It is from Death — "his
truer name is Onward," he says — that Tennyson draws the promise of the solution hereafter. The great argument which he gradually
opens out in " In Memoriam " he sums up again
in the concluding words of " Vastness : " —

" I loved him, and love him forever : the dead are not dead,
   but alive."

That is to say that the love which he bore to
his friend, and again to his son, did not die
with their deaths, but still lives, and will live
forever. This undying love is to him a witness
that its object is actually living, too, in spite
of what Death may seem to say to the contrary. For that apparent contradiction is but
the shadow, while the reality is to be found in
the Sun of Life towards which Death's face is
looking. And if this experience, this conviction, be true, and if there is a love and a life
stronger and more lasting than death, then

there is a Lord of Life who rules all this world by perfect love. When we have gone into that world of light, then and there the mystery will be made clear.

Foster. He has crossed the bar, and put out to sea on that voyage of discovery : let us hope that he has found his Pilot in the ship, able and ready to carry him to the harbor where he would be.

The Squire. I cannot doubt it. It is pleasant to think how often that image of a voyage and a harbor has presented itself to all sorts of men. Cicero makes Cato, after speaking of this life as a mere inn, compare that future life, to which he so earnestly looked forward, to the harbor at the end of the voyage. Sa'di, quoting, I think, from the Koran, says, "He who has Noah for a pilot need not fear the waves of the sea." And if you will forgive the garrulousness of an old man, I may add a little experience of my own, which comes back to me as often as I recall Tennyson's verses on "Crossing the Bar."

Foster. What is that?

The Squire. In the old days before there were any railways in Italy, most of us who went to Naples went by way of steamer from Marseilles ; and it was at the end of November, seven-and-thirty years ago, that I took passage in such a steamer. All day there had raged

one of those gales of wind and rain which
sweep the plains of Provence and the Gulf of
Lyons with such terrible fury. But no delay
more than of a few hours was possible, and
we were required to embark at midnight. The
water seemed smooth as we went into the
ship in the port; but as we crossed the bar
and put out to sea, the leap into the utterly
black night of wind and waves and rain was
terrific. I could not see our pilot face to face;
but I knew that he was there through all that
long night and day, and that on his skill it
depended whether we should reach the harbor
where we would be. At last I slept, while the
storm still raged. When I awoke we were in
smooth water, through which our ship was
gliding on with an imperceptible motion, along
that lovely scene of mountains and islands,
and vineyards, orange orchards, and olive
woods, which open out into the Bay of Naples.
The day was breaking, the sun was rising
upon that land of beauty, and the cloudless
depth of the blue sky was reflected in the not
less intense blue of the sea.

Foster. I know that sight, and cannot wonder that the Neapolitans themselves should
call it a piece of heaven fallen upon earth, or
say that he who has seen it may die content.
But you said just now that Tennyson is our
greatest teacher in the matter of the Sphinx's

riddle : do you put him above Frederick Maurice, of whom you often speak as the greatest teacher of our generation ?

The Squire. No. Each stands first in his own plane of thought and life ; but I should rather put them side by side than either above the other. Each learnt, and knew that he learnt, much from the other. Each of them — the poet and the prophet alike — felt and knew himself to be a man sent from God, and that the calling and the mission of both were essentially the same. Maurice was primarily a teacher of the gospel ; but while he never ceased to declare the good tidings of a Kingdom of God in and for itself, he recognized its pervading presence in every form and every relation of man's life, to which it gave a new and higher worth and meaning. Tennyson, on the other hand, shows us earth and man as they are in themselves, with all their complications and interfusions of good and evil, happiness and misery, vice and virtue, and then finds himself obliged — drawn as it were by an irresistible intuition — to look out of and above this earth for a clue through its contradictions into a true order.

Foster. Certainly it is so. Few of the greatest poets, in any age or country, have been irreligious ; most have been religious, recognizing a government of the world by God.

But even among Christian poets of the higher
order of genius, I can think of no one who
rests on the faith of another life than this
so distinctly as Tennyson does. To eliminate
this faith from Tennyson's poetry would indeed be to reduce it to dust and ashes. What
would "In Memoriam" or the parting of
Arthur and Guinevere, "Crossing the Bar" or
"The Two Voices," be without it?

The Squire. You see this distinction if you
compare Wordsworth with Tennyson. Wordsworth was a Christian in faith as well as life,
and his mind was formed in and through the
great burst of enthusiastic belief in the per-
fectibility of human nature to which all generous spirits gave themselves up in the later
years of the eighteenth century. In many
respects he shared to the full in the general
reaction which followed on the excesses of
the French Revolution; he became a Tory,
and he wrote the "Ecclesiastical Sonnets."
But his mind retained much of its first bias.
You see this in "The Excursion," where, while
admitting and allowing for the moral and the
bodily ills of the society and the human nature
generally around him, he looks forward to
universal education of the people by the state
as the sufficient remedy for all the evil. We
have the education, and it is well worth
having; but I suppose few expect from it

now what Wordsworth expected. I, at least, look with Tennyson for a remedy different in kind, and not merely in degree.

Foster. Was Maurice a man of letters as well as a theologian?

The Squire. He would have liked to be called a man of action better than by either of the other names. But he was a true lover of books, and he always seemed to me to know everything about every book and every writer of books, in his own day or in times past. His literary culture was greater than that of most men, — you see the evidence of this in every one of his books; and I believe that he who himself knows most of other men's books will know most of the use which Maurice made of books, not as mere storehouses of facts or thought, but as supplying the memory and mind with a knowledge and a culture which were all his own. But with him literature and literary culture were means to an end, and not the end itself. He always spoke with scornful contempt of the fine gentlemen of letters; and you may remember a letter of his to a pupil, — with whom, by the bye, he had been reading Plato, — urging him to make politics the main study of his life.

Foster. But I suppose he was a political philosopher rather than a politician?

The Squire. He would not have thanked

you for telling him so. He would indeed have
told you that philosophy being the search after
wisdom, politics, like everything else, should
be an object of that search. But he despised
the habit of mind which affects to rise above
party politics while really sinking below them.
He was a keen and eager politician on all the
great questions of the day, though he was
sometimes on one side and sometimes on the
other. The earliest of his tracts in political
controversy was in defense of university sub-
scription to the Thirty-Nine Articles, but he
was found in hearty sympathy with Lord John
Russell's abolition of all such tests. He was
a leader in the struggle to keep the education
of the nation in the hands of the Church, but
he heartily approved Mr. Forster's Education
Act. He recognized that the time had come
for the disestablishment of the Irish Church,
notwithstanding his filial love for the like
institution in England. And while I recall his
predicting to me, more than fifty years ago,
and with warm political sympathy, the future
eminence of the then unknown but strong
conservative Mr. Gladstone, I recall also his
appearance, thirty years afterwards, as the
supporter of John Mill, the radical candidate
for Westminster. These are brief instances of
what the man was ; and all through, no one
who knew him could doubt either his honesty

or his consistency, as he looked in succession at the many ways in which the progress of the world was fulfilling itself.

Foster.

> " We might discuss the Northern sin
> Which made a selfish war begin ;
>   Dispute the claims, arrange the chances ;
> Emperor, Ottoman, which shall win :
>
> " Or whether war's avenging rod
> Shall lash all Europe into blood."

The Squire. I always thought that Tennyson and Maurice lost their heads a little over the Crimean war, as most other people did ; and I have therefore been inclined to suppose, though without any authority for doing so, that when the excitement was over they looked back on it, as did Lord Aberdeen, the minister who let us drift into it, as not only a blunder, but a crime.

Foster. Yet I have heard German statesmen say that they owe to that war the loosening from their necks of the yoke of Russian policy and diplomacy under which they had so long groaned.

The Squire. No doubt some good was done in that way, but they would not touch the roasting chestnuts with their own fingers.

Foster. Well, at least the war gave us "The Charge of the Light Brigade;" and though I do not mean to compare Sir Francis Doyle with

Tennyson, perhaps one might say his no less fine ballad upon the same subject.

The Squire. They are fine ballads, and bring out finely the English soldier's ideal of duty as the rule of his life. But those who, like me, remember the sufferings not only of the army through that terrible winter, but also of the wives and mothers at home, may think the price high, even for two such songs.

Foster (humming half to himself).

> " If I were King of France,
>   Or, still better, Pope of Rome,
>   I'd have no fighting men abroad,
>   No weeping maids at home."

But, Squire, are you really for peace at any price? I remember what you once wrote in approval of the extermination of the Canaanites by the children of Israel and of the soldier's duty, taught not only at the Pass of Thermopylæ, but in the Balaclava charge.

The Squire. No, not at any price, but at almost any price, as Sir John Lubbock said the other day in the House of Commons. For every nation there exists a real danger of attacks, from within or without, on its laws and liberties ; and it is not only its right, but its duty, to defend itself, and sometimes its weaker neighbors too, against such attacks. If we cannot keep our national life, with its laws and its freedom, without war, let us have war;

but let us not go into it "with a light heart," talking glibly of honor and spirit on the one hand, and of humiliation and shop-keeping on the other. I am old enough to remember when even many a wise and good man talked that sort of stuff about dueling, and really believed that it was a moral duty to shoot, or be shot by, any ruffian who called him a liar or struck him. No one says or thinks that now, and ruffianism has abated, not increased, in proportion.

Foster. Is it not the fact that all the great nations of the world, modern as well as ancient, have had their foundations laid by war, and that they have been from time to time enlarged and strengthened and invigorated by means of war, and all this in such a way that we cannot conceive how the results could have been brought about except by war?

The Squire. As I said just now, I do not deny the existence of evil, nor the still more mysterious fact that it is inconceivable how many of the highest forms of moral good could have been brought into existence except by means of evil. I neither understand nor deny, but I will not call evil good for all that. War has brought into existence soldiers like Chaucer's " Knight," Wordsworth's " Happy Warrior," and Schiller's " Max Piccolomini ;" but they have been but few in comparison with the countless swarms of ruffians licensed for murder, robbery, and lust. And free as the German army was from all these crimes in the late Franco-German war, it is said that after the war was over there was an increase in crime throughout Germany which could be explained only by the general demoralization which the war had produced.

Foster. The other day you quoted from the Persian poet Sa'di that it had been said that, in the last great day, the All-Merciful would forgive the bad for the sake of the good ; but now you seem to hold that all the good must be condemned on account of the bad. I think of what the world would have been in the past and present, and what the world would be in the future, with no England and no United States, and I ask myself whether too high a price was paid for these in the Anglo-Saxon and Norman conquests, the wars of the barons and of the king and Parliament, or in the American wars of independence and emancipation.

The Squire. With reservation of Friday's theological difficulty, I agree with you not only ungrudgingly, but with hearty sympathy. I believe the price was not too great. But was the price necessary in the past, and will it be so in the future ? I say, Yes, men being what they were ; but, No, men being what they

ought to be and well may be now. It is better
to do a good thing badly than not to do it at
all ; but it is better still to do it well. We talk
too much about necessary evils, and think too
little of necessary good ; forgetting that all
good is possible, and that in every case what
is possible is necessary. In this matter of war,
as in so many other things, successive generations, advancing in the possession of ever fuller
national life, with its rights and liberties, find
many necessary evils to be unnecessary, and
much more impossible good to be possible.
And so, if you will grant the evils of war, and
I its good, we may be able, like Dogberry and
Verges, to "draw to a point."

Foster. Did Maurice change or modify his
views on this subject?

The Squire. He has discussed this question
of war in the eleventh of his Cambridge Lectures on Social Morality, published in 1869, to
which I would refer you. But I can tell you
a little incident, trivial in itself, yet perhaps
interesting when told of a great man. No one
shared more eagerly than did Maurice in the
outbreak of enthusiasm with which the war
was hailed at first. When I ventured to doubt
the righteousness of the war, he declared, with
indignation, that only the Spirit of God could
stir up and maintain such a national enthusiasm as the English people were then showing,

I suppose we agreed to differ, and not to
argue. I do not think I asked him what he
thought of that to me pathetic account of the
regiments of Russian conscripts having hardly
arrived at the seat of war from very distant
parts of the empire when, at two o'clock in the
morning of that cold day of November, all the
church bells of Sevastopol rang out, and these
men, having received the sacrament, went to
die for their Czar in the lines of Inkerman.
But after the war was over, I was breakfasting
with Maurice, and there met a man who told
the story of the Balaclava charge as he had
lately heard it from one of the officers in it.
He said the cursing and swearing of the
troopers as they rode into and out of the
Russian battery were awful. And I guessed
what thoughts might be passing through my
friend's mind when he said, with that quiet
and almost sad seriousness which so often
characterized his words and manner, "I am
afraid many things in that war happened
differently from what we supposed," — or
words to that effect.

Foster. I should have thought, as I now
think, of Uncle Toby and his account of our
soldiers in Flanders. I think, too, of the tear
of the recording angel. The poor fellows were
doing their duty, and their profane swearing
did not mean much more than any other form

of battle shout. I do not recollect the mention of shouting in modern stories of battles, but soldiers do shout in a charge, do they not?

The Squire. Sir William Napier, the historian of the Peninsular war, told a cousin of mine, Charles Buller, that it was the British shout which carried the day in our great battles; nothing could withstand it. Of course, the shout is the man; he utters what is in him. I remember that Marshal MacMahon, when comparing the soldiers of different nations, said, "The English do not understand campaigning, but they are the best on the day of battle." We have wandered far, however, and I do not wish you to think that when my dear old friend and I met, either in this house or in his own, our talk was of nothing but soldiers. With him as with Tennyson, he would always

> "turn to dearer matters,
> Dear to the man that is dear to God;

> "How best to help the slender store,
> How mend the dwellings of the poor;
> How gain in life, as life advances,
> Valor and charity more and more."

Foster. Yet there is something of the soldier's desire for action implied in the poet's description in those words; and I can fancy that with Maurice the heart of the man of thought would always warm to the man of action.

The Squire. Yes ; Maurice must have understood how Luther — with whom he had, indeed, many points of likeness — felt when he was going into the Diet of Worms, and the old soldier, Georg von Freundsberg, called out to him, " Monk, monk, you have before you such a day's work as neither I nor our bravest captains have seen in our hardest fought battles. But if your cause is just, go forward boldly : God will not forsake you." Maurice wrote two books which will live, for they are full of learning, thought and genius, — "The Kingdom of Christ," and "Moral and Metaphysical Philosophy ;" but he expressed the temper of his whole life when he once said to me that a man might bring greater honor to his name by writing a great book, — I think he instanced Gibbon, — yet that he believed more real work was done in the world by having a part in, and writing on, the actual controversies of the day in which men were taking a practical interest. And though it was after he said this that he wrote the two books I have mentioned, you may see by the number, and still more by the subjects, of the many volumes of his collected works how fully he carried out through his life the principles he had laid down for himself.

Foster. Is Dickinson's portrait like him ?

The Squire. I think so, but it is difficult

to know how far I may be reading into it my own recollections of the man himself. There it is, and you may try it by my description. His face was very fine and delicate in feature ; the expression was saintly, though not quite the ascetic saintliness which characterizes some of the portraits of great men of the Roman Catholic Church ; it was rather tinged with the sweet, homely humorousness which you see in Cranach's portrait of Luther. The eyes were bright and piercing, and the mouth was firm and compressed. The whole expression of the face was energetic, almost aggressive, and yet kind and gentle : it was the look of a man who had a message to give, and who was resolved to give it ; but the resoluteness had more of self-sacrifice than of self-assertion in it.

Foster. You spoke of a humorous expression. Was he a humorist ?

The Squire. You could not be long in his company without seeing how strong his sense of humor was ; but, like every man of humor who is wiser and better than a humorist, he kept his love of humor within the limits of becoming mirth ; nay, within limits which were habitually serious, often almost to sadness.

Foster. He had a fine voice, had he not ?

The Squire. A grand, deep voice, well fitted to pour out the volume of thought and feeling

behind it. Bunsen said to hear him read the
prayers at Lincoln's Inn, where he was chap-
lain, was in itself to hear a sermon ; and some
one else said, still more expressively, that he
prayed the prayers. I remember the out-
spoken delight of one of the cottagers as we
came out of the church here when Maurice
had been preaching. It reminded me of the
story of the learned Pococke, of which he
(Maurice) was fond : that when a friend, visiting him at his country parish, asked one of
the villagers how they liked their new parson,
the answer was, " He is not much of a Latiner,
but he tells us what we poor folks want to
know about God and Jesus Christ."

Foster. Nullum tetegit quod non ornavit,
— would you say that of his conversation generally?

The Squire. He was shy and retiring, — a
lamb among the lions, as a lady described him
at a great party of Mrs. Charles Buller's. He
was free from the foible of omniscience attributed to one of his Cambridge contemporaries,
and far above the vanity of the good talker.
But no one could listen to him for five minutes
without perceiving that no ordinary man was
speaking. In serious controversy and with
his pen in his hand he hit very hard. I used
to tell him that he reminded me of a story of
his own, how, when he was a young curate, he

stopped in the High Street in Leamington to remonstrate with a man who was belaboring his donkey furiously, when the man replied in an appealing voice, "Why is he so stupid, then?"

Foster. What does Tennyson refer to in those lines at the beginning of his "Invitation," about giving the fiend his due, and the anathemas of college councils?

The Squire. You will find the whole story in Colonel Maurice's admirable life of his father; but it was, shortly, this: Maurice denounced the irreligious spirit of the so-called religious newspapers, and they retaliated by not only denouncing him, but also warning the authorities of King's College that they had better dismiss him from his professorship of divinity in that college. A packed council was convened, a lately published essay in which the professor had "given the fiend his due" was made the pretext, and Maurice was dismissed, in the face of the clearest evidence that he had maintained nothing contrary to the acknowledged doctrines of the English Church. Maurice was one of the very few men whom I have known as lovers of justice for its own sake; yet he got little justice himself on that occasion. But the rain is over; let us take a walk, and leave Jim to keep his paws warm at the fire.

VII.

RIDING DOWN TO CAMELOT.

The Knight's bones are dust,
And his good sword rust : —
His soul is with the saints, I trust.

COLERIDGE.

THE Squire was from home for a day or two, on business. When he came back, he asked the ladies, "What have you been doing while I was away?" They answered, "We took Mr. Foster to Camelot, to convince him that it was Cadbury in Somersetshire, and not Winchester, which he declared Caxton to have said it to be."

The Squire. Caxton was a wise as well as a good man, and his knowledge was great; but even he did not know everything. In the Introduction to the Globe Edition of " Morte Darthur" you will find the reasons for holding that King Arthur's Camelot — probably from Camelus, the Celtic god of war — was the Cadbury Castle you saw yesterday. But perhaps you are already convinced that you had seen the true Camelot, and that Arthur really held his court there?

Foster. Certainly. I felt like Mopsa, who loved a ballad in print, because then she knew it to be true.

The Squire. I should like to hear your account of the expedition. I know you keep a journal.

Foster (fetches a notebook, and reads from it). "We got to Sparkford at about one o'clock on a day of terrible midsummer heat; from there we drove to South Cadbury, about two miles off. The drive was across a plain; in fact, the end of the great valley which runs up from the sea, roughly speaking, bounded by the Mendip range on one side, and the Polden hills, parallel to Mendip, on the other, and the beginning of the downs which join on to the system of Salisbury Plain, shutting in the valley at right angles to Mendip and the Polden Hills. In this great trench are islands: near the sea, such ones as Brent Knoll; further up, Glastonbury Tor; and furthest from the sea, and just under the downs, lies Camelot. As we drove, we could see, looking towards our right, the downs bounding the horizon with their characteristic slopes, the flat tops and steep sloping sides and general plainness of surface which give to downs an individuality among hills. Along their ridges were to be seen scars on their sides, showing old encampments. Close under these downs stands Camelot, a long, regularly sloped hill, quite isolated, its top at a distance looking nearly horizontal, while the two ends present a slope of about the same angle; the side towards us was thickly wooded, and so no ramparts were to be seen. At South Cadbury, a pretty village, with its little church and pollard poplar-trees round it, we began our walk. A narrow lane, with steep banks, leading out of the highroad, and called Castle Lane, began to go up the hill. After a short distance we reached a gate: here the lane widened, and seemed to go straight up the hill in a broad ditch. A short way up, roads branched to right and left; on the one to the left was a gamekeeper's cottage. These branching roads were, in fact, the first ditches at the top of the first slope of earthwork. Before telling of our ascent of the fort, I will describe the general lines on which the defenses are made, as this will simplify the account I am going to give of the details. Imagine to yourself a plain out of which rises a hill, two hundred feet high of regular shape; on the northern side a slight slope up from the plain suddenly turns into a steep rampart of about fifty feet, so steep that we, like Camden, found it easier to run down it than walk. Gaining the top of this first rampart, you find yourself on a narrow edge, sloping steeply down to a ditch, a slope of perhaps ten feet; from the bottom of this ditch rises the second rampart, of about the same height as the first, which again ends in an edge sloping down to a second ditch, from which rises the third rampart, like the second, but not so high as the first and second, though as steep; this, too, has its ditch, and from it rises the fourth and last rampart. The top of this one is embanked about ten feet above the nearly flat top of the hill. This is a space of some twenty acres, and at the eastern end enters the roadway leading up from the bottom to where I have said we first began to climb, the roadway cutting through ditches and ramparts. This entrance was, no doubt, protected by the iron gates which still live in tradition. So the road enters the oval top of the hill at the eastern end. Opposite, at the western end, another road just like this one comes up from the bottom; a little to the north of this western gate the ground rises in a knoll, called Arthur's Castle, and is the highest part of the hill, being five hundred feet above the sea. It has steep sides, which seem partly the result of art, and partly natural.

"One could not help being struck by the simple earth walls and their primitive strength, and feeling how different must have been the people who lived here in rude strength from the gorgeous images of the Camelot of Malory. How entirely the life here must have differed from the mediæval surroundings from which he drew his color! And we could not help wondering who were the people who began to make a fortress out of the hill, and what were the names of those who had brought these earth mounds and ditches to such perfection of strength. Strange that the genius that planned and the energy that executed should have left only the work accomplished, and no record of those by whose might it was framed! Strange that a people so great, who could carve the everlasting hills into citadels, and whose mounds and ditches have survived 'the drums and tramplings of three conquests,' [1] should have left no name even in the histories of nations now dead!

" 'But the iniquity of oblivion blindly scattereth her poppy, and deals with the memory of men without distinction to merit of perpetuity. Who can but pity the founder of the Pyramids? Herostratus lives that burnt the temple of Diana; he is almost lost that built it.' [1]

The greater part of the hill is wooded. This, unfortunately, hides the ramparts and ditches, except at close quarters, but then they are seen clearly. We made our way up

[1] Sir Thomas Browne, *Urn Burial.*

through the eastern entrance, walked across
the oval top, and went out at the western gate
down the hill to the bottom, where we found a
wall below the last rampart shutting in the hill
from the fields round. We then walked round
the northern slope inside this wall, in search
of the Wishing Well. After going a little way,
the Squire's daughter saw a cow " —

The Squire (interrupting). And you all ran
for your lives, I suppose?

Foster. No, we did not. The young lady
only availed herself, as her father would have
done, of the opportunity for the exercise of the
higher criticism, as you will see if you let me
go on, — " saw a cow on the top of the first
rampart above us (here not very high), and
thought this might indicate water. We went
to the place only to find a muddy pool, and
were thinking of going on farther, when the
other lady of the party, her sister-in-law, noticed, a little to the right of the pool, a few
steps above it, a small inclosure some twenty
feet square, made by a low, dry wall; going
into this, she found the well. The second
rampart slopes up at the back of the little
inclosure, making one of its walls; in its side,
on the ground, is the Wishing Well. A block
of stone, about four feet long, has been hol-
lowed out into a circular arch, the inside of
which is cut into a scallop shell; this block

might be the top part or roof of a semicircular niche, though here it rests on no pillars, but the ground, so the opening is only some two feet high and three long; the surface of the water was about a foot below the ground, in a little basin built, apparently, of brick, on the same plan as the scalloped roof, — that is, in front straight, the back a half-round. The water was as clear as crystal, and of icy coldness. Although the shape of the stone was evidently not very old, possibly of the time of Queen Anne, as it is sometimes called Queen Anne's Well, still, here it seemed a living thing of the past. The soft gurgle of the spring, as it ran away in some hidden channel, heard only when one bent close to the water, made one feel it was thus that this spring ran when those ramparts over our heads, now slumbering in peaceful decay, had resounded to the busy life of a capital city of the old British kingdom, or had echoed to the battle cry of a mightier race, the torrent of whose conquest this citadel had stayed, but not arrested. Not only did the well put us in touch with 'the clouded forms of long past history,' but we also thought of those whom poets have made much clearer.

> " ' Feigned of old or fabled since,
> Of faery damsels met in forest wide
> By Knights of Logres or of Lyones,
> Lancelot of Pelleas or Pellenore.'

For, at Camelot, Arthur and his knights still
ride at the full moon and water their horses at
this well. The hill of ramparts and ditches
rose in the imagination to something much
more than a stockaded camp of a savage tribe,
and, like Leland before us, we felt that we
were at the local habitation of those airy no-
things, those fancies of poets' brains, King
Arthur and his Knights of the Round Table,
whose deeds had played as important a part
as had Troy the ancient, and influenced the
modern world as greatly. Whether it was from
such thoughts as these or not I cannot say,
but the water of the Wishing Well seemed a
draught inspiring beyond all other water. But
we had other things to see yet, and above all
to prove if the hill were hollow; for the
legends of the country assert that a noise
made at King Arthur's Well is heard at the
Wishing Well; so the ladies stayed at the
latter, while I started in search of King Arthur's Well, the other spring on the hill. This
I found at no great distance, close to the
cottage, and on the left side of the eastern
road up the hill. There was a stone with a
round hole in it about two feet across, the well
below being a circular place about four feet
deep, full of filthy and all but stagnant water,
and quite powerless to excite the imagination.
At the appointed time I made much noise by

hitting boards and sticks on the mouth of the
well; but on going back to the Wishing Well
found that my noises had not been heard.
Considering that we had drunk deep of the
clear spring, I was relieved to think it did
not communicate with the poisonous waters of
King Arthur's Well. We now set out to see
more of the southern side, and, walking along
past the cottage, found ourselves on the top
of the first rampart. On the southeastern
slope the walls of earth stand out in bald
grandeur, for there are no trees, and here we
could appreciate the enormous strength of the
ramparts rising tier above tier over our heads.
I have seen other camps of this kind, but
never anything like this; the steepness of the
sides and the regularity of the slopes make it
a striking spectacle. As we got farther round
on the south side, trees began again, though
more scattered; and as we climbed up gradually, startling countless rabbits, and at one
place a badger, the views became of great
beauty, till, reaching the top of the southern
side, near the west gate, we looked down on
the village of Sutton Montis. Nothing could
have been more lovely. A little brook with
willows skirted the fortress, after leaving the
downs opposite whence it rose; across this
brook lay a vast orchard, the orderly rows of
its great trees clearly seen from our height;

beyond this came the 'pleasant villages and
farms adjoined,' — one especially glowing roof
of almost crimson tiles took the eye ; beyond
this, again, the church, and then the vast
sweep of view towards Dorsetshire. From
here we went through the western gate of the
top of the camp, and descended the hill by the
road at that end, leaving Camelot by the west,
having come there by the east. We then went
a pleasant way across the grounds, orchards,
and fields, till a path near the river took us
back into Sparkford, where the interval till
our train was due was filled by many cups of
tea in a pleasant old inn. The train took us
home in a golden evening, and we were left
with visions of romance and of the monumental
handiwork of a vanished people, all seen
through a halo of midsummer sunlight."[1]

The Squire. Very good geography, physical,
military, and archæological ; not without a
touch, too, of purple patch, and some of a
very fine purple.

Foster. If it had been full moon or the eve
of St. John, I think I should have begged the
ladies to stay with me, or to leave me there,
that I, too, might hear and see Arthur and his
knights come riding down King Arthur's Lane,
as, according to local tradition, they have

---

[1] An account of an actual visit, by my son, Mr. Henry
Strachey.

never left off doing since the days of Leland,
whose account I have just being reading, who
tells us of the silver horseshoe that one of
them had cast in such a ride.

The Squire. I have often fancied that if I
had the poet's gift of looking into and seeing
the imaginary past, while the senses of the
present are laid asleep, the vision would come
to me on the grassy mound called Arthur's
Castle, at the top of the hill of Camelot. Even
now that vision rises before me with successive
magic scenes, "apart from place, withholding
time," but always in that golden prime of
Arthur and his knights. I seem to see the
town of Camelot, while within the hall is the
Round Table, its seats filling with knights
come to the feast of Pentecost, though Arthur
will not take his place till he hears from Sir
Kay, the Seneschal, that an adventure is at
hand, since some unknown lady or knight can
be seen riding down the road. Scene after
scene rises before me of things done, and
words spoken, and quests undertaken, in that
hall ; and not least that when the Holy Grail,
covered with white samite, passed through,
offering every knight for once to partake of
that mysterious food, and awaking in him the
resolve to achieve that quest. And then,

"I see no longer, I myself am there,"

among the crowd of ladies and knights who

gathered to see the barge which came floating down the river with the dead but beautiful Elaine, the Lady of Shalott, and hear Sir Launcelot tell her sad tale. The river may be seen by the bodily eye, and in the light of summer day; and so may Glastonbury and Avalon, no longer, indeed, an island on the one hand, and the site at least of the nunnery of Almesbury on the other. But now the vision rises before me of the twofold story of Malory and Tennyson, of that parting, solemn to awfulness, of Arthur and Guenever, when he rode out through the mist, without looking back, to the battle which he knew was to be his last; of the battle, and of the coming of that barge with the weeping ladies who bore away the dying king to Avalon. Then, again, those last laments of Launcelot over Arthur and Guenever, and of Ector over Launcelot himself. These actions are very real to me; and yet, as I speak, I know, like Prospero, that they are melting into air, into thin air.

Foster. My sympathies are all with you, Squire, but yet forgive me if I ask, as I heard your little grandson ask the other day when you were telling him a story, " Is it true? Tell me something real." And I should be glad to think that the fabric of your vision is not altogether baseless, and that there was an Arthur after all. Milton, with all his admiration for

Arthur and his knights as heroes of romance, did not believe in his historical existence ; so you will hardly expect me to satisfy my doubts by the historical arguments with which Caxton tells us that many noble and divers gentlemen satisfied his doubts, nor even by the evidence which they called in of Gawain's skull, Cradock's mantle, and Launcelot's sword.

The Squire. Though you took his word for it that Camelot was Winchester. But I can give you better authority than that of Caxton, or Milton. Here (opening a drawer, and taking out a letter) is the last letter which I received from my old friend Edward Freeman. He writes : —

"Guest taught me to believe in Arthur, and there is a notice of him which, if not history, is at best very early legend, in the Life of Gildas. It proves a good bit, anyhow. Then Rhys seemed to disbelieve in him, and now he seems to have taken to him again. I tell Rhys that I live much too near to Avalon, which is Glastonbury, to give him up altogether, and that I can't part with him to them of Strathclyde."

Foster. Gildas does not mention Arthur.

The Squire. No ; but what I understood Freeman to mean is this : Agreeing with Green in acknowledging the great authority of Guest as to the history of this period, he takes the

time of comparative peace and prosperity which
Gildas describes to have been that of the
reign of Arthur between 520 and 542. The
resistance which Arthur more or less success-
fully maintained during his life was renewed
after the battle of Deorham in 577, and not
finally overcome by the Saxons till the battle
of Penna in 658. And it is reasonable to suppose this long resistance was in part made
possible by the support of the line of fortresses
of which Camelot was the chief and centre.

You will find the still later conclusions of
Professor Rhys in his learned volume "The
Arthurian Legend" and his Preface to Messrs.
Dents' Edition of "Le Morte Darthur."

But it is a very slight and dim existence at
best. You just now compared the story of
Arthur to that of Agamemnon ; and I might
add that Camelot is to Malory's "Morte Darthur" what Dr. Schliemann's Troy is to the
Iliad.

Foster. Why then did you say they were
melting into thin air ?

The Squire. I cannot say so, after all.
Those knights and ladies do live to me, as I
trust that they will live to many an English-
speaking boy and girl yet unborn. But I will
answer your question in the best Dryasdust
fashion that I can. I do not attempt to follow
up the old legends to those pre-Christian and

even prehistoric sources of which some learned
writers believe that they can get occasional
glimpses. I am content to believe that in
the ages in which war was more to men than
peace, and imagination more than cool reason,
the legends somehow grew up. The British
bards termed the actual losses of their countrymen glorious gain and triumphs of poetry; and
when they were driven back into Cornwall and
Wales and Scotland, they found everywhere
new Camelots and Round Tables at Tintagel,
Caerleon, and Carlisle, and across the sea in
Brittany. Mr. Symonds tells us that in the
Middle Ages the legends of Arthur were
greater favorites with the educated classes in
Italy than the earlier ones of Charlemagne,
which were left to the common people. And
it is a curious fact that Gervase of Tilbury,
writing early in the thirteenth century, gives
a story of the discovery in the woods of Mount
Etna, in Sicily, of King Arthur, there biding
his time in solemn seclusion, which exactly
corresponds with the like story which has been
told of the Somersetshire Camelot by a peas-
ant girl to a lady, now living. The minstrel,
or troubadour, wandered far; and he carried
everywhere with him not only the name, but
the local habitation of his hero.

Foster. Were not the Chivalry romances
chiefly French?

The Squire. If you except the greatest of all, that of Sir Thomas Malory, perhaps they were. He says there were in Welsh many, and in French many; and he also makes use of old English romances. But the Curate found in Don Quixote's library a pretty good number of Spanish romances. And you must remember that French was the language of the English Norman lords and ladies, and that England was first of the lands of chivalry, whatever was its chief language.

Foster. I think Southey says, in the preface either to his " Amadis " or " Palmerin," that the Spanish and Portuguese romances bear evidence, in their references to England, that this was so.

The Squire. I like to see significance in the fact, pointed out by Frederick Maurice, that the man whom the Germans, the French, the Italians, and the Spaniards honored as ritter, chevalier, cavaliere, caballero, the rider of the war horse, was to the English the knight, the knecht, the servant of all men.

Foster. Is not Amadis of Gaul the most perfect embodiment of the ideal of knighthood? He is as pure as Perceval or even Galahad, without their monk-like asceticism; and as true and ardent a lover as Launcelot, without his guilty " honor rooted in dishonor," as Tennyson calls it.

The Squire. The loves of Amadis and Oriana are, indeed, charming. There is nothing in Malory like that description of them in Southey's translation : —

"Oriana was about ten years old, the fairest creature that ever was seen ; therefore she was called the one 'without a peer.' The Child of the Sea (that is, Amadis) was now twelve years old, but in stature and size he seemed fifteen, and he served the queen ; but now that Oriana was there, the queen gave her the Child of the Sea, that he should serve her, and Oriana said 'that it pleased her ;' and that word which she said, the Child kept in his heart, so that he never lost it from his memory, and in all his life he was never weary of serving her, and his heart was surrendered to her ; and this love lasted as long as they lasted, for as well as he loved her did she also love him. But the Child of the Sea, who knew nothing of her love, thought himself presumptuous to have placed his thoughts on her, and dared not speak to her ; and she, who loved him in her heart, was careful not to speak more with him than with another ; but their eyes delighted to reveal to the heart what was the thing on earth that they loved best, and now the time came that he thought he could take arms if he were knighted ; and this he greatly desired, thinking that he would do such things that, if he lived, his mistress should esteem him."

I often feel the force of the arguments of the worthy Ascham against the tales of chivalry, and wish that Malory had made Amadis, and not Launcelot, his principal hero. But then I recur to what Caxton had written long before, as if in anticipation of the charge, and how Tennyson has brought out, in full life and proportion as well as with the lineaments of the noblest poetry, this contrast between good and evil, and triumph of good over evil, which Caxton eulogizes in Malory's story.

Foster. Milton, too, while he expresses a pious and thankful wonder that his youthful footsteps should have been directed in the paths of chastity by the tales of chivalry, among which Malory's "Morte Darthur" no doubt found a chief place, seems to recognize that the moral effect on his young mind had been good, and not evil.

The Squire. The growth and progress of moral life are as marked and worthy of notice in our tales of chivalry as in any other form of our civilization. And it was our happy lot that, just at the right time, a William Caxton was ready to print and publish the great national epic which he had found and encouraged a Sir Thomas Malory to write. Like the Iliad, it is partly of that lofty and serious kind in which the imagination can believe and find enjoyment. A little later, the old tales of chivalry could only have supplied the material for a moral allegory like that of the " Faerie Queene," or a genial burlesque like that of "Don Quixote," or a hard, cynical, political satire like that of " Hudibras."

Foster. You have said nothing of Tennyson's revival, may I say, of the old faith in the old poems. It is true, they are idyls, little pictures, and you call Sir Thomas Malory's romance an epic. Do you hold to that eulogistic designation of Malory's " Morte Darthur," in face of the half-patronizing, half-contemptuous language in which the Caxtons of the present day have described the very book on which they have just lavished all the learning, labor, and cost of many years, — a work which very few will care for or appreciate at its proper value, though many may enjoy the popular fruits of it all ?

The Squire. So it is, and must be. I have the sincerest respect for a learning, industry, and generous self-devotion to the cause of letters such as I can make little pretension to. But while I know enough of these things to appreciate what these scholars have done for us, I see no proofs that I ought to submit myself to their authority on a question on which it contradicts my own literary judgment.

Look at this book of Malory's, "Morte Darthur," as it actually is, and not as the critics
say it ought to have been, if he had properly
followed his sources. You will find on every
page the marks of a work of true though early
and somewhat rude art; and then, if you will
look again with your own eyes, and not with
those of the critics, you will see that his art
is all his own, and not to be found in the older
legends which he has used as materials. I do
not know whether Malory had acquaintance
with any of what have been called the masterpieces of antiquity, nor whether he was conscious at all that he was himself creating one
of such masterpieces. But his work itself lies
before us. He has taken the legends of an
old national hero and fashioned them into a
work of art, with the main characteristic
features of the epic, or the drama, of all ages
and countries. It is what Carlyle would have
called the perennial battle between God and
the devil, — the contest between man's free
will and his circumstances ; the Nemesis which
attends his way during that contest, and his
triumph by help of a higher power than his
own. Διὸς δ'ἐτελείετο βουλή. Arthur is born
into a world of anarchy, for which the law-
lessness of his father is more or less responsi-
ble ; Merlin watches over him, and, by help of
his counsels, Arthur, on reaching manhood, is

able to establish and consolidate his kingdom, and even to extend it over that of the Emperor of Rome ; and the Round Table at which he sat as the centre and head of his knights was the sign and token of this world under kingship. But there was a canker at the root of all this glory. After many years of prosperity and of great deeds, both good and evil, the coming of the Holy Grail brought a test which could not be escaped ; the fellowship of the Round Table was broken up, and Mordred, the child of the guilty loves of Arthur and Morgan le Fay long years before, became the instrument of divine judgment and retribution. Thus the personages of the story, through whose action its several threads are woven or unwound, are as artistically varied and distinguished as are the events. Both these points of the story and the characters are discussed at some length in the Introduction to the Globe Edition of "Morte Darthur," to which I may refer you, if you care for more. Only for the humor of it, do read me the account of the Bishop of Canterbury's excommunication of Mordred. You will find a mark at the page.

Foster. "And then came the Bishop of Canterbury, the which was a noble clerk and an holy man, and thus he said to Sir Mordred : Sir, what will ye do, will ye first displease God, and sithen shame yourself and all knighthood? Is not King Arthur your Uncle, no further but your mother's brother, and are not ye his son, therefore how may ye wed your father's wife? Sir, saith the noble clerk, leave this opinion, or else I shall curse you with book, and bell, and candle. Do thy worst, said Sir Mordred, wit thou well I shall defy thee. Sir, said the Bishop, and wit you well I shall not fear me to do that me ought to do. Also where ye noise where my lord Arthur is slain, and that is not so, and therefore ye will make a foul work in this land. Peace, thou false priest, said Sir Mordred, for and thou chafe me any more, I shall strike off thy head. So the Bishop departed, and did the curseing in the most orgulous wise that might be done. And then Sir Mordred sought the Bishop of Canterbury for to have slain him. Then the Bishop fled, and took part of his goods with him, and went nigh unto Glastonbury, and there he was as priest hermit in a chapel, and lived in poverty and in holy prayers: for well he understood that mischievous war was at hand."

The Squire. That touch of the bishop escaping into a humble and quiet hermitage, but prudently taking some of his goods with him, after he had done the cursing in the most orgulous manner, always strikes me as very happy. Sir Thomas Malory was a humorist;

but his pathos is greater than his humor.   Let
us hear those last words of Sir Launcelot and
Sir Ector.   One can never be weary of them.

Foster (reads).   " Truly, said Sir Launcelot,
I trust I do not displease God, for He knoweth
mine intent, for my sorrow was not, nor is not,
for any rejoicing of sin, but my sorrow may
never have end.   For when I remember of her
beauty and of her noblesse, that was both with
her King and with her ; so when I saw his
corpse and her corpse so lie together, truly
mine heart would not serve to sustain my
careful body.   Also when I remember me how,
by my default, mine orgule, and my pride, that
they were both laid full low, that were peerless
that ever was living of Christian people, wit
you well, said Sir Launcelot, this remembered,
of their kindness and mine unkindness, sank
so to my heart, that I might not sustain myself."

And again : —

" Ah, Launcelot, he said, thou were the
head of all Christian knights ; and now I dare
say, said Sir Ector, thou Sir Launcelot, there
thou liest, that thou were never matched of
earthly knight's hand ; and thou were the
courtliest knight that ever bare shield ; and
thou were the truest friend to thy lover that
ever bestrode horse, and thou were the truest
lover of a sinful man that ever loved woman ;

and thou were kindest man that ever strake with sword; and thou were the goodliest person ever came among press of knights; and thou was the meekest man and the gentlest that ever ate in hall among ladies; and thou were the sternest knight to thy mortal foe that ever put spear in the rest."

The Squire. Here again I would refer you to the Globe Introduction for proof that in these and other instances the passages are either Malory's own, or have been converted by him into poetry out of mere prosaic materials. In his twenty-first, or last book, in which I think his art is at its highest, he frequently alters or changes the incidents from those in the French books which he is always quoting; and in each case it seems to me that the variation has been made for the sake of artistic effect.

Foster. You call "Morte Darthur" a poem, then, and Malory a poet?

The Squire. He has the poet's eye to see into the life of things, and the poet's power to endow what he sees with outward form and color, but he wanted that essential qualification of the proper poet which Wordsworth calls the accomplishment of verse.

Foster. Did not Carlyle say that poetry would be better if it were written in prose instead of in verse, and that it might be hoped that the poetry of the future would be so written?

The Squire. I suppose we are all more ready to justify than to confess our mental deficiencies; and though Carlyle had much poetic insight, he had not the poet's proper faculty of expression.

Foster. How would you define this poetical mode of expression? It is something more or other than the skillful art of making lines of ten syllables with or without rhymes at the end.

The Squire. One characteristic — I had almost said *the* characteristic — of verse, in the highest meaning of the word, is its reticence. It was said of the great linguist, Cardinal Mezzofanti, that he could keep silence in forty languages; and the poet is a man who can and does keep silence in the midst of his wealth of rushing thoughts and words; and it is in this accomplishment of verse that he finds that the limitations of verse make this silence both proper and profitable. His words must be few, while and because every one of them must be a creation, a cosmos, in itself, pregnant with life and meaning. Tennyson evidently saw and understood this in the formation of his style, — in part cultivated his poet's art which makes his style, in the highest sense of the word, and in which it has been well said

to be the man himself. Mr. Knowles tells us [1]
that he said "'Wordsworth would have been
much finer if he had written much less;' and
he told Browning in my presence that 'if he
had got rid of two thirds, the remaining third
would be much finer.' After saying that, and
when Browning had left us, he enlarged on the
imperative necessity of restraint in art. 'It is
necessary to respect the limits,' he said. 'An
artist is one who recognizes bounds to his work
as a necessity, and does not overflow illimit-
ably to all extent about a matter. I soon
found that if I meant to make any mark at all
it must be by shortness, for all the men before
me had been so diffuse, and all the big things
had been done. To get the workmanship as
nearly perfect as possible is the best chance
for going down the stream of time. A small
vessel on fine lines is likely to float further
than a great raft.'"

Foster. And so you contrast these small
vessels, the "Idylls," with Malory's great raft
of "Le Morte Darthur"?

The Squire. Yes. And if you like to shift
the metaphor from the ship to the river, you
may quote Denham and say:—

> "Oh, could I flow like thee, and make thy stream
> My great example as it is my theme!
> Though deep, yet clear; though gentle, yet not dull;
> Strong without rage; without o'erflowing, full."

[1] *Nineteenth Century* for January, 1893.

Each generation has its own authorities and
teachers. I quote Tennyson now; fifty years
ago I thought Coleridge's distinctions of poetry
and romance, prose and verse, the best possible; and indeed I think you will still find
them worth reading.

Foster. I know them well, though I did not
read them fifty years ago. Judged by Coleridge's standard, is not Malory's book a romance rather than a poem?

The Squire. Perhaps it is. I am not at all
willing, even for Malory's sake, to break down
the distinction between prose and verse which
I think so real and so important. I will content myself with saying that it is a work of art,
real though rude; and for this I have the
voice of the world of letters, gentle and simple,
on my side, the few and minute critics notwithstanding. Whatever sidelights their learning
may have supplied to Spenser, Milton, and
Tennyson, there can be no reasonable doubt
that the Arthur and his knights whom they knew
are the king and knights of Malory. The popular
voice of approval has never been silent since
Caxton printed his first edition; and during
the present century it has been raised, with an
ever-increasing volume, to what Tennyson may
be said to have given a not inappropriate expression when he said, "There is no grander
subject in the world than King Arthur."

Foster. The bibliography of the book is curious and interesting, especially as to Upcott's very ingenious interpolations to supply the missing pages of the Althorp copy. It seems odd that the truth had remained undiscovered for fifty years till you told the story in the Introduction to the Globe Edition.

The Squire. When I came to look into the history of the text for myself, I was astonished at the inaccuracy and slovenliness of the professional critics, and their habit of putting second-hand guesses in the place of verified facts. But I venture to say that you may depend on the bibliography of the Globe Introduction and the Prolegomena of Dr. Sommer. The work of Dr. Sommer is, indeed, a wonderful monument of German learning, industry, and contentment with the reward of the approval and admiration of the few scholars competent to judge of its merits.

Foster. I am afraid that you cannot include the authorities of the British Museum among those who justly appreciate the worth of Malory's book, when they allowed the one perfect copy of the original edition to go to America.

The Squire. From what I have heard, I guess that they outwitted themselves by the overdone caution — not uncommon with buyers at auctions — of trying to make their purchase

without giving their bidding agent a free hand.
I was very sorry when I first heard that the
precious volume which, when it lay in the
Osterly Park library, had been seen by very
few but myself, was gone to Brooklyn instead
of to Bloomsbury. But I could no longer
grudge the loss when I remembered that the
treasure had only gone to our brothers — may
I say our sister? — across the Atlantic, with
whom, as its possessor, Mrs. Abby E. Pope,
tells me, it is prized more than it was among
ourselves. I could only wish that it may be
as safe from risks of fire and other damage as
it would have been in the British Museum,
and that the present possessor of the Althorp
copy will obtain — as would no doubt be allowed — a photograph facsimile of the missing
pages, to be substituted for the very inaccurate
though beautifully written transcript by Whit-
taker. But here comes tea. Queen Guenever
and her ladies never poured out that at the
Round Table, nor invited Arthur and his
knights to "five o'clocker."

VIII.

THE ARROWHEADED INSCRIPTIONS.

The dust of a vanished race.

TENNYSON.

I KNEW that the Squire took much interest in the Arrowheaded Inscriptions, so one morning I got him to talk on the subject.

Foster. Do you read the Arrowheaded Inscriptions of which I see so many volumes?

The Squire. No; I content myself with enjoying the fruits of other men's labors; hoping, however, that I may occasionally get from these learned men some new light on questions which may not have attracted their own attention.

Foster. Scholars now quote the records of Rameses and Sennacherib as much of course as they do the Commentaries of Cæsar; but the discovery of the key to the decipherment of the Egyptian hieroglyphics and the arrowheaded inscriptions must have seemed very wonderful at first, as indeed it was.

The Squire. Yes. These keys, like photography, with the silver plate of Daguerre fol-

lowed by the paper-printing of Talbot; the
electric telegraph, with its development of the
telephone and the phonograph ; and I may
add, the uses of steam by sea and land, — all
these are now every-day things. Yet I can
recollect something of the sense of the marvel-
ous which fell upon some of us on their first
discovery. It seemed a happiness only to
have lived in those days, to borrow a phrase
from Wordsworth about the early days of the
French Revolution : only we, happily, have not
had to repent, as he had to do.

Foster. The reading of the Egyptian hieroglyphics seems comparatively easy, if I rightly
remember the account of the process. Was
it not that the French, in 1799, found at
Rosetta a stone with an inscription of Ptolemy
Euergetes in Greek and in the demotic or
common Egyptian writing of the period, as
well as in hieroglyphics? And then, by assuming that the vernacular Egyptian of the time
of the inscription did not differ materially from
the Coptic of the present day, it was found
that Coptic equivalents for the several words
of the Greek could be made out and read
in the demotic version, so that finally the
hieroglyphic inscription itself could be read.
But then Ptolemy, like Pharaoh, had told his
dream to the wise men, who had to interpret
it. Nebuchadnezzar needed to be told his

dream as well as the interpretation thereof. There was no inscription, in Greek or any other known language, was there, at Persepolis or Behistun?

The Squire. On the contrary: Diodorus said the Behistun inscription was by Semiramis, and Rawlinson found it to be by Darius. You are right in the main as to the comparative easiness of the hieroglyphic decipherment, I think, but in both cases the discoverers must have possessed and exercised no small amount of the powers of criticism and divination, which Niebuhr calls the means by which history supplies the deficiencies of its sources. But the decipherment of the arrowheaded inscriptions was no doubt by far the more difficult; and its results have, in my opinion, far surpassed the other in their interest and historical importance.

Foster. I know less about the arrowheaded than about the hieroglyphic inscriptions, and shall be glad if you will tell me something about them.

The Squire. The subject is a vast one, and it continues to increase. I will show you the few pebbles I have picked up on the shore; but if I exhaust your patience, it will not be by the knowledge of the learned Dr. Dryasdust who has recorded all that has been done or written on the subject. I have only the odds

and ends which I have gathered up through
many years from journals of learned societies,
books of translations, monographs on fresh
discoveries of lions and bulls and bricks and
slabs, and so on in infinite variety.

Foster. It is a pleasant way of getting knowledge, if only a man's memory can keep all
that he so collects ; but

> "Time hath, my lord, a wallet at his back
> Wherein he puts alms for oblivion."

The Squire. No; I will, like Time, in this
case quote the general at the siege of the
impregnable fortress of Bhurtpore, when he
had ordered a gun up to a particular position.
The officer came back, after some time, and
reported that it was impossible. "Impossible,
sir! Why, I have the order in my pocket!"
So the gun was brought up, and the fort was
taken. There, at Persepolis, for two thousand
years had stood that rock, rising four hundred
feet above the plain, with its scarped face
covered with writing which no man could read,
and so looking foolishly enough, as Carlyle
said of the Pyramids. The imaginative in-
habitants of the land, forgetting that their own
fathers had written and read those words,
believed them to be the work of jins, telling
of hidden hoards of gold and jewels never to
be discovered, while some wise skeptic from
the West pronounced them to be merely the

work of worms. But there, age after age, still
stood the old General Time, with the order in
his pocket, waiting for the hour and the man.
The beginnings of the discovery were humble
and its progress was slow, but we may say that
the critic and the diviner were there from the
first with Philology, Archæology, and History
for their tools to work with. Increasing in-
telligence and accuracy in copying the inscription were followed by increasing recognition of
the arrangements, repetitions, and variations of
the still unknown characters. They were in
three columns, of which there were in one
only forty-two of the little groups of arrowheads or wedges, each of which groups might
be assumed to be a letter; in another column
there were four hundred of such groups, which
therefore must have been ideographic: and
these characters and signs, for which ample
space was taken at one end of the line, were
crowded together at the other, thus showing
that the writing was from left to right. From
each of these facts was derived an hypothesis,
which, when verified, became the law of a new
hypothesis, to be verified and expanded again
in like manner. If these columns were used
for a proclamation by a king ruling over the
country in which they stood as a centre, the
three columns were probably the same proclamation in the three principal languages of

the monarchy, like those which the Sultan of
Constantinople or the Shah of Persia still
issues in Turkish, Arabic, and Persian. It
might be taken that, being at Persepolis, this
proclamation was by some king of the once
great Persian Empire; that the language of
one of its columns would be the Persian of the
time: and that, with the unchanging customs
and habits of the East, the style of his proclamation would most likely be the same as
that used by the Sassanian dynasty which
reigned in Persia till the Muhammedan conquest. The languages of the columns with
the letters or signs counted by hundreds were
clearly what we call ideographic, like those of
the Chinese or the Egyptians, in which each
character represents a mental image; while the
writing of the column with only forty-two variations of character was as plainly phonetic,
in which each sign was merely a letter of an
alphabet, as with ourselves. By these steps,
Grotefend, in 1802, reached his position: the
right-hand column is in alphabetical writing,
and, assuming it to be a proclamation in the
Sassanian form, beginning with the name of a
king who calls himself king of kings, and son
of a king with another name and the same
title. Now, as to the inscription beginning
with three words differing from one another,
but combined with three other words, these

repeated twice, the third being the same as the second, with an additional letter or letters, — I cannot put my hand on Grotefend's paper, but I understand his reasoning to be something of this kind: Call the three first-mentioned words A, B, and C, and the sentence will run thus: A, king of kings, son of B, king of kings, son of C. The word read as *king* is repeated with an addition which indicates the genitive plural, while the other repeated word stands for *son*. But C is not called "king of kings," like the other two. Then the three names are Xerxes, Darius, and Hystaspes; for the last, though father of Darius, was not a king. But to say that certain words meant *son* or *king* was not to read the words themselves, or to say to what language they belonged. Now, however, the Zend, or ancient Persian, began to be studied, and it became possible to say what those words would be if all the other assumptions were true. The other letters were hypothetically added to those which made up the names of the three kings. If Zend were the language in which the inscription was written, the words for *son* and *king of kings* would be *putra* and *kshayathiya*, and more letters of the alphabet would be added to those in the three kings' names. So the inscription was gradually read, found to agree with the story of Herodotus, and

took its place among the records of ancient
Persia.

Foster. And so a key was found, like that
of the Greek version on the Rosetta stone, for
reading the other Persepolis inscriptions, one
of which was, I suppose, Assyrian ?

The Squire. The actual course of things
was somewhat different. Colonel (afterwards
Sir Henry) Rawlinson, containing in himself,
in no common degree and in very various
kinds, the qualifications of a man of action
and of letters, had become so familiar with
arrowheaded writing, which he had studied at
Persepolis, that it seems as if it had been a
sort of mother tongue to him, when he says
that he cannot remember and trace back the
steps by which he arrived at his knowledge.
On visiting Behistun, he was able to read the
Persian column of the trilingual inscription
there found, and to tell the world that it was
a proclamation, not of Semiramis, as Diodorus
had supposed, but of Darius. A copy of the
text with a translation was sent to England
by Rawlinson, and published in the Journal
of the Asiatic Society in 1847. To employ
this deciphered inscription for the purpose of
reading the other inscriptions side by side
with it might have been interesting to Rawlinson in any case, but a new motive for such
work had arisen. Botta in 1847, and Layard

in 1845, had discovered, by actual excavation, the vast remains of the palaces of Nineveh and other cities of Assyria, the existence of which, under great earth mounds, had been conjectured by King in 1818. These excavations were the beginning of a work which is still going on; of the discovery not only of the remains of magnificent buildings, but of an almost infinite variety of written records in the arrowheaded characters. There were not only monumental inscriptions on colossal bulls and lions, and on alabaster slabs which had lined the walls of the palaces, but also on clay tablets of every size, which had been baked after the arrowheads had been impressed on them, and which tablets were eventually (as I will explain directly) found to be books of all sorts. The characters in which all these were written were recognized as those of one of the trilingual inscriptions of Persepolis and Behistun; the genius which had read the Persian inscription of Behistun must have found it comparatively easy to read the Assyrian column, while employing Hebrew, just as Zend had been employed in the previous case, at each step of hypothesis and verification. And in 1852 Rawlinson was able to send home from Nineveh the Assyrian annals of Sargon and Sennacherib themselves, whom we had till then known of only from the

Hebrew history, and the still scantier Greek records. There were at first many failures and hitches, and learned men looked more or less doubtfully on the popular enthusiasm at a discovery which came home to every one who had read the Bible. Some years later a challenge was given, and accepted by Rawlinson, Hincks, Talbot, and Oppert, to translate independently of one another an inscription of which the untranslated original had been published by the British Museum; and to submit this to the judgment of Sir George Cornwall Lewis, Dean Milman, and Mr. Grote. The versions substantially agreed, except as to the proper names; but, if I remember rightly, Sir George Lewis remained incredulous, and Mr. Grote not quite satisfied. The key to the special mystery of these and other proper names was eventually found; and I suppose that no one now has doubts that those who are at the trouble may learn to read Assyrian as they do Greek or Sanskrit.

Foster. A library of brickbats for books sounds funny. It must have required some courage to begin reading in it.

The Squire. Yes; and especially when the books lay in heaps by the thousand, having, as Mr. George Smith conjectured, fallen with the ruins of the building, from an upper floor.

Foster. You alluded to other special difficulties in the way of decipherment; what were they?

The Squire. If I have rightly read the earlier work in the fuller light of the later knowledge, the story is something of this kind: The Assyrians were in the main a Semitic people; their language, like their race, was allied to that of the Hebrews, and their writing, like the Hebrew, was alphabetical. But the older civilization of Babylon, from which Assyria derived much of its own, was Turanian, and its method of writing was not alphabetic, but ideographic, like that of the Chinese and several other peoples. The Assyrians, very oddly, as it seems to us, combined the two methods, using dictionaries for the purpose, some of which have been actually found in what you call the library of brickbats.

Foster. Can you give me an example?

The Squire. Here is one which I took many years ago. The Roman letter and numeral X is for many purposes an English ideograph, or character, used to express, in writing, not a mere sound, but a mental image. In a date we read it *ten;* after a king's name, *the tenth;* between two figures, as 3×3, we read it indifferently as *times, into,* or *multiplied by;* the mathematician uses it as *an unknown quantity;* and the stockbroker reads Xdiv. as *without the dividend.* No one hesitates to read Xway

as *crossway;* and though X only represents a
syllable in Xmas, Xtian, and like words, here,
too, it may be called an ideograph. But now
suppose that, in addition to all these uses of
X in writing, we employed it also to express
the sound of *ten* without attaching any mental
image to it, and in any word in which that
sound occurred as one of its joints, as in
tenant, tender, tent, we indifferently wrote the
full word in alphabetic letters, or substituted
X for t-e-n, and so with Xant, Xder, Xt. Imagine this double method of expressing what
I call a joint, or joints, in a word employed
habitually, and with every variety of ideographic sign drawn from the Babylonian ideographic writing, and you have the usual Assyrian method of writing. This may serve as
an illustration, though it is of course only a
small and fragmentary one, of what was a very
complicated business, though no doubt it was
easy to those accustomed to it. But, as I have
said, they used dictionaries or lists of ideographic characters with their equivalents in
Assyrian letters.

Foster. Was it from these dictionaries that
the way to read the strange forms embodied in
half-spelt words was found out?

The Squire. No. I think the first discovery
was by help of one of those happy accidents
which come to men of genius, and which they

know how to seize and make their own. An inscription was found in duplicate. In one copy Rawlinson came to a word which, if read phonetically and as if the language were He-brew, gave good sense ; in the other copy, this word was expressed by one which, if so read, would give no sense, and was in fact no word. This, then, was the ideographic equivalent of the real word. The clue was followed, and the labyrinth was traversed in and out. If you would explore the matter farther, you must put yourself under the guidance of Rawlinson, Schrader, Sayce, and George Smith ; and in-deed I might easily add other names.

Foster. It is curious that while the Hebrews were using leather and the Egyptians papyrus to write on, the Assyrians should have used clay.

The Squire. It is fortunate that they did so. They did, however, also use some perishable material, no doubt leather ; for seals have been found with the holes for the strings which fastened them to the scrolls, and even the remains of the strings themselves. These seals are of clay, often with two impressions, one of which has Phœnician characters, showing them to belong to contracts between two parties. Some of these deeds of sale between Phœ-nician and Assyrian traders have also been found, and have helped to throw light on the question of language. But the most interesting of all the seals is one which bears the Egyptian hieroglyphics which had been already read by Egyptologists as the name Sabaco II., king of Egypt, and also an Assyrian device of a priest ministering before the king, which is reasonably supposed to be the royal signet of Sennacherib, the contemporary of Sabaco. It is manifestly the seal of a treaty between these two monarchs whom we know to have met in battle not many miles from Jerusalem.

Foster. Has the discovery of Egyptian and Assyrian records given much help in the study of Hebrew history and literature?

The Squire. A good many facts, more or less important, and much general light, in which the old facts may be seen more plainly than before. A second history, especially if it be a contemporary history, always gives a greater sense of reality to the first one. One of the uses of two eyes is that each eye sees a little more of one side of the object than does the other ; and thus the object is seen to be, what it is, a solid, and not a flat object. A photograph represents an object as seen with one eye ; and when two such photographs are brought together into one picture by the stereoscope, we immediately perceive an effect of roundness instead of flatness. We may and do know that an object is solid, though we look at it with only one eye, but we only *see* it to be so when we look at it with both. Critics with the historical imagination of Grotius and Gesenius could infer and make out from the discourses of Isaiah the military and political position of Jerusalem when its little territory was becoming the battlefield on which the rival monarchies of Egypt and Assyria met to fight for empire. But the picture is made still more lifelike when, alongside of the actual speeches by which Isaiah sustained and directed the energies of his king and countrymen in the supreme hour, are read the annals in which Sennacherib tells what he and his army were doing at the same time, within the sight of the men who, from the walls of the city, could see the valleys and plain full of Assyrian horsemen.

Foster. And besides these military and political annals, are there not some considerable remains of literature of the kind which reflects the general moral and intellectual culture of a nation?

The Squire. Yes, and these, too, throw much light on the history and literature of the Jews. Now that we know that the people of Israel, at the period to which they carried back the life of their national ancestor Abraham, were in the midst of nations which had not only reached a high degree of civilization, but knew

how to record that civilization in writing, we
should be wholly unreasonable if we doubted
the claim of the Jews to the possession of
equally early written records. The old orthodox belief that Moses was miraculously
enabled to write the Pentateuch, and the
preposterous modern adaptation of the old
rabbinical legend that it was the work of Ezra
after his return from the exile, are equally
unnecessary.

Foster. Are you not rather unfair to these
modern critics? I recollect a J and E as well
as a P C in the list of what I suppose you
would call their imaginary documents. And
then, is not "preposterous" rather a strong,
or, as Jeremy Bentham would have said, "dys-
logistic" word?

The Squire. When Burke was called to
order for using the word "preposterous" in
one of his speeches in the Warren Hastings
trial, he justified himself by observing that the
word only meant putting the cart before the
horse. I cannot but think that this is a common habit of mind in our modern Biblical
critics; though I respect the wonderful minute-
ness and industry of their learning, and have
no doubt that it often throws new light on the
subject they treat of.

Foster. Then you do not accept as con-
clusive the decision of Professor Wellhausen

that the Old Testament, as we have it, was edited and published in the year 444 B. C.?

The Squire. I know that a German professor is, like the prophet Habakkuk in the opinion of Voltaire, and the father of a family according to Napoleon, "*capable de tout.*" Yet I have looked at that date again and again, and wondered how any one could believe it possible to evolve out of his inner consciousness the exact year, more than twenty-three centuries ago, of an event of which there is no record that it happened at all; and why that odd number of 4, or even 44, when dealing with so many hundreds, and even thousands? I can only compare this conscientious accuracy to that of the man who refused to imperil his immortal soul by saying that he had killed the round number of an hundred canvas-back ducks when in fact it was only ninety-nine.

Foster. But, Squire, you just now quoted with approval Niebuhr's two qualifications for the historian, — criticism and divination. Will you not allow his countrymen and their English followers the use of these things in the study of Hebrew literature?

The Squire. If they only would use them more than they do! The true critic is a judge. His business is to bring all the ascertainable facts of the case into clear light and order,

and then either to pronounce a judgment, or
to declare that no judgment is possible for
want of sufficient evidence. He is not, in the
latter case, to make up the deficiency by
fancies drawn from his inner consciousness to
supply the lack of facts.

Foster. Is not this the divination of Niebuhr?

The Squire. No, no. I believe Niebuhr
himself may have sometimes mistaken the one
for the other, but they are not the same thing.
Divination in history is seeing into the life of
things, not the dissection of a dead body and
the labeling of the several parts. But there is
another saying of Niebuhr's which is more to
the point. He says that when in Rome you
may often see existing walls with marble frag-
ments of columns and cornices built into
them ; and it is certain that these are the
portions of some older buildings, temples or
palaces perhaps, but it is impossible to say
what those buildings were. A like illustration
might be drawn from some of our old churches
and manor houses ; and we know what woeful
work our own learned modern architects have
made of their so-called restoration of these.
The churchwardens' whitewash has done far
less harm. I have no difficulty in seeing, with
Astruc, the plain marks in Genesis of two
records, marked by the names of Elohim and

Jehovah respectively; but I cannot follow Wellhausen in the ideal reconstruction of his so-called prophetic and priestly documents elaborated out of the early books, and duly docketed J E and P C.

Foster. I see your shelves full of the commentators you so scoff at.

The Squire. I not only respect, but profit by their learning and industry, which are very great. I gladly use their books, though I do not like to wear their chains. There are some words of Grote on a like question in Greek literature which deserve to be written in letters of gold, and to be ever before the eyes of the student of the Old Testament. He says: "The lesson must be learnt, hard and painful though it be, that no imaginable reach of critical acumen will of itself enable us to discriminate fancy from reality in the absence of a tolerable stock of evidence. . . . In truth, our means of knowledge are so limited, that no man can produce arguments sufficiently cogent to contend against opposing preconceptions, and it creates a painful sentiment of diffidence when we use expressions of equal and absolute persuasion with which the two opposite conclusions have been advanced."

Foster.

    " And art thou nothing? Such thou art as when
    The woodman winding westward up the glen

At wintry dawn, where o'er the sheep-track's maze
The viewless snow-mist weaves a glist'ning haze,
Sees all before him, gliding without tread,
An image with a glory round its head.
The enamored rustic worships its fair hues,
Nor knows he makes the shadow he pursues."

It seems a pity; is nothing left for us but this luminous mist?

The Squire. The books themselves; read the commentaries with them. You will not understand the books without their help. Only, read the commentaries for the sake of the books, and not the books for the sake of the commentaries, as has been always, and still is, the habit of too many, from the days of the Talmud, and before, down to our own.

Foster. You remind me of Bacon's advice : " Read not to contradict and confute, nor to believe and take for granted, nor to find talk and discourse, but to weigh and consider."

The Squire. You can have no better instruction for the use of the commentaries. And for the books themselves, the more you read them for their own sake, the more you will find worth reading in them. People often think it clever to say that the Bible should be treated like other books. I wish it got a little more such treatment. Those who believe that it really differs in some respects from other books ought to be the most convinced that the more clearly you bring out the resemblances,

the more distinctly will the differences come
out, too.   Read the books as they are, and let
the likenesses and the unlikenesses come out
as they may.

Foster. Will you give me some illustration
of your method?   I will ask no questions as
to the authorship of the book of Genesis, but
what do you say of its account of the Creation,
when the modern sciences of astronomy, geology, and ethnology have shown us that the
beginnings of all things are lost in infinite
distances of time and place?

The Squire. Whatever discoveries the mind
of man has made in all these directions, — and
I do not question their reality or their importance, — they have neither satisfied nor
even ascertained man's demand for some ideal
of a Creation, the work of a Creator.   And
this is just what the Hebrew story of the
Creation supplies.   David Hume, lifting his
eyes to the sky on a starry night, said to
Adam Ferguson, "Oh, Adam, how can a man
look at that and not believe in a God!"   Some
three thousand years before, the same faith
was perhaps awakened by the same sight in
the mind of the Hebrew, whoever he was.
The institutions of his country had accustomed
him to think of work and duty with the rules
of law and order as the highest and noblest
forms of life, and therefore those ideals in

which his belief in a Creator must centre itself. It must be work and it must be good, worthy of the highest workman. But there are method, law, and order in all the higher kinds of work. One of the most ancient of his national institutions, held to have been given to his people by the Divine King himself, was that work was regulated by the week, — the division of time into six days of work and one of rest.

Foster. Then do you go on to discuss such questions as whether these days in Genesis are actual days or geological periods; and if the latter, whether they have any claim to represent accurately those periods in our modern science?

The Squire. I repeat that I certainly like to read such disquisitions, but not either to contradict and confute, nor to believe and follow. I prefer the treatment of Seneca and Cicero, of Addison and Wordsworth, as well as that of the Hebrew psalmists and prophets themselves. There is, too, if I remember rightly, a fine passage in Luther's Commentary on Genesis to the like effect. The concrete forms of the imagination are not less natural than our logical or scientific abstractions, and are much more needful to our moral life. And when you show me that Hebrew imagination and modern science and logic do not run together exactly on all fours, and that there

has been no miraculous interposition to give
the first the same kind of accuracy as belongs
to the others, I say, so much the better. Logical skepticism, like that of Hume and John
Mill, recognizes the conceivableness of a
miracle where there is a reasonable ground
for expecting it; but here the account of
Creation is all the more human because it in
no way anticipates Newton's " Principia " or
Lyell's " Principles of Geology." Nor is any
claim it may have to be held to be super-
human affected by the showing that it is not
preter- or non-human.

Foster. Do not the readers of the arrowheaded inscriptions find that the Assyrians
divided the lunar month into four weeks, with
days of rest named the Sabbath, and an account of the Creation in six days?

The Squire. We are told so, with other
things of a like kind. If they were confirmed,
they suggest the question whether the Hebrew
traditions, which are so infinitely nobler in
moral and intellectual as well as literary character, are developments of the ruder and
coarser beliefs, or are themselves the older,
and were afterwards degraded from their earlier simplicity. The Hebrew account of the
migration of their traditional ancestor, Abraham, will fall in with either supposition. The
germs of national life, civil and religious,

which he brought with him, and which eventually grew into so great a tree, may have been mere germs, or they may have already grown up somewhat, though in very inferior forms, in Babylon and Assyria. The question is interesting, yet it is perhaps incapable of any answer but what the individual habit of mind of the inquirer may give it.

Foster. I understand you, then, to hold that there is so little evidence as to the early or late date of the Hebrew books, and so much probable, at least plausible argument on either side, that the reasonable course is to keep the mind in suspense on the subject. I like to hear both sides; and yet when I have heard one, I always feel like the judge who, when he had heard the plaintiff, stopped the case, because he said he saw it very clearly as it was, and should only be puzzled if he heard more.

The Squire. So do I; but there is no help for it. Anyhow, these prose epics of the Hebrews keep their ground, age after age, in all lands: and that because, for simplicity, pathos, grandeur, and, in a word, humanity, there is nothing equal to them. They, and not Latin and Greek, are the *literæ humaniores* of the world. Milton was a competent judge, for he knew all alike, and he expressed his preference for the Hebrew above all other literatures. Of its lyric poetry, after speaking, in the preface to his second book on the "Reason of Church Government," of "those magnific odes wherein Pindarus and Callimachus are in most things worthy," he says, "But those frequent songs throughout the Law and the Prophets, beyond all these, not in their divine argument alone, but in the very critical art of composition, may be easily made to appear, over all the kinds of lyric poetry, to be incomparable."

Foster. Does Milton anywhere speak of the book of Job?

The Squire. I do not remember that he does. He calls the Song of Solomon a pastoral drama; and no one would have gainsaid him if he had declared that the book of Job embodies in the purest poetry the true idea of the tragic drama, — the riddle of the Sphinx of Greek tragedy. And then you know as well as I do his comparison of the Hebrew poets and prophets with the Greek and Roman poets and orators. But let me hear you read what one can never be tired of.

Foster (reads).

> "Or, if I would delight my private hours
> With music or with poem, where so soon
> As in our native language can I find
> That solace? All our law and story strew'd
> With hymns, our psalms with artful terms inscrib'd,
> Our Hebrew songs and harps, in Babylon

That pleased so well our victor's ear, declare
That rather Greece from us these arts derived;
Ill imitated, while they loudest sing
The vices of their deities, and their own
In fable, hymn, or song, so personating
Their gods ridiculous, and themselves past shame.
Remove their swelling epithets, thick laid
As varnish on a harlot's cheek, the rest,
Thin sown with aught of profit or delight,
Will far be found unworthy to compare
With Sion's songs, to all true taste excelling,
Where God is praised aright, and godlike men,
The Holiest of Holies, and his saints;
Such are from God inspir'd, not such from thee,
Unless where moral virtue is express'd
By light of nature not in all quite lost.
Their orators thou then extoll'st, as those
The top of eloquence; statists indeed,
And lovers of their country, as may seem;
But herein to our prophets far beneath,
As men divinely taught, and better teaching
The solid rules of civil government
In their majestic, unaffected style,
Than all the oratory of Greece and Rome.
In them is plainest taught, and easiest learnt,
What makes a nation happy, and keeps it so,
What ruins kingdoms and lays cities flat;
These only with our law best form a king."

Do you think that their political philosophy was so instructive and important as he says?

The Squire. I have written a volume to try to answer the question, Yes, as to one of the prophets, Isaiah. But still I continue to ask it of myself. My doubt is less whether it is true than how and when it can and will be shown to be true. Our political morality is not very high; yet we live and move, if only half consciously, in a religious atmosphere unknown to the Greeks and Romans, but without which we could not breathe. And this atmosphere is the belief in the God made known to the Hebrews in the plain of Mamre and the Temple of Jerusalem.

Foster. I suppose the differences and contrasts between the Jewish and the Assyrian religions are greater than their resemblances?

The Squire. Infinitely greater. There is much simplicity in the Jewish ritual, notwithstanding the daily Temple services, which stands in marked contrast to the swarms of gods, devils, and spirits of all kinds, good and bad, with the rites and ceremonies appropriate to them all. It is indeed a puzzle how great military conquerors like Tiglath-Pileser, Sargon, and Sennacherib could have found time for them.

Foster. I suppose it was chiefly a mechanical work which their priests could do for them, —a sort of live praying-machine, not essentially different from the Tibet praying-machines, which they work, as travelers tell us, by hand or by water-power, for private or public worship, as the case may be. But Isaiah speaks of these conquerors as if they had no religion at all, but were mere atheists.

The Squire. Not unnaturally, though a nine-

teenth-century philosopher like yourself may
know better.   But I am reminded of a curious
parallel between the language in which Sennacherib describes his treatment of Merodach-
Baladan, king of Babylon, and that of Isaiah
as to the fashion of the conquest of one of
Sennacherib's predecessors.   The Assyrian
king says, "All his broad country I swept like
a mighty whirlwind.   Over their cornfields I
sowed thistles."   "He himself — for the fury
of my attack overwhelmed him — lost heart,
and like a bird fled away alone, and his place
of refuge could not be found."   And the Jewish prophet I might almost say rejoins, though
his words are a little earlier in date, "For he
saith, By the strength of my hand I have done
it, and by my wisdom ; for I am prudent : and
I have removed the bounds of the people ; . . .
and as one gathereth eggs that are left, have
I gathered all the earth ; and there was none
that moved the wing, or opened the mouth, or
peeped."

Foster.   Should you say that the Assyrians
had much civilization, in an ordinary use of
the word ?

The Squire.   Possibly as much as the Romans had before they conquered Greece.   Like
the Romans, they loved great public works ;
and the remains of their buildings amply con-
firm us in supposing that Sennacherib said

truly, "Of all the kings of former days, . . .
though the central palace was too small to be
their royal residence, none had the knowledge
nor the wish to improve it. . . . Then I, Sennacherib, . . . by command of the gods resolved
in my heart to complete this work." From
this and other passages it is evident that
Sennacherib was what the Romans called a
great ædile. Then the Assyrians kept historical Annals of the Empire, the truth of which
is proved by their records of eclipses, which
have been verified by modern astronomers.

Foster. But, granting without reserve that
our Assyriologists have really recovered the
language and read the inscriptions, are we
bound to believe all they tell us of the poetry,
religion, and literature of this ancient country
as fluently as if they were giving us an account
of modern China or Japan?

The Squire. Hafiz says that the leader of
the caravan cannot be without information
about the road and the customs of the wayside
halting-places; and these learned men must
know much more than we, and be able, as we
are not, to look at things with eyes trained to
use in twilight. On the other hand, it is not
unreasonable to suppose that they may a little
overrate what has been in fact a very wonderful discovery, or series of discoveries. I confess that when reading in good modern English

the Assyrian story of the Creation or the Deluge, I have felt a certain relief, a sense of having a bit of firm ground under my feet, when I have come to the statement that from here the tablets are missing, or some lines of the writing are so mutilated as to defy decipherment.

Foster. Like Sidney Smith's admiration for Macaulay's occasional flashes of silence. But I am sure you will be glad of more than a flash of silence after all this long talk.

IX.

TAKING LEAVE.

There 's no use in weeping
Though we are condemned to part:
There 's such a thing as keeping
A remembrance in one's heart.

CHARLOTTE BRONTË.

I WAS recalled to town, and had to bring my pleasant Somersetshire visit to an end. When I told the Squire, he said, "I am sorry you must go; but a good host must speed the parting as well as welcome the coming guest. We have not had much to show you, except the humors of the general election. I hope you have not found your visit dull."

Foster. Far from it. I have seen and heard so much that I wish I could sit down to look round and consider a little before I make my last day's march, like the soldier in the French story which one of the ladies read to us the other day.

The Squire. You mean the description of the soldier returning home, who stops, when in sight of his native village, to look back on his past service before he finishes his concluding march. It is one of Émile Souvestre's idyls,

— little pictures, — which are always so charming; but it ought to suit me rather than you, as it is the opening of his " Souvenirs d'un Vieillard." Old age comes in every variety of form. There are all sorts of men, soldiers, statesmen, men of business, of letters, of science, and peasants, who die in harness. There are some men and women whose powers of body decay, while their minds keep, or even add to, their original vigor; with others the mind — or perhaps it is really the brain — goes before the body; while with others, again, there is a gradual and gentle decline of the powers of action both of mind and body to the last. And though we all instinctively feel death to be an evil for ourselves and for those who love us, yet a man may live too long, or at least till his life seems to have no further use than to point the moral that death is not only inevitable, but no less natural than life, so far as this world is concerned.

Foster. You remind me of Swift's horrible picture of the Struldbrugs.

The Squire. The caricature is frightful, but the likeness cannot be denied. It would be better for us all, for ourselves as well as for the young men in whose way we stand, if we old men took Swift's warning more to heart; for the old man to die in harness is for the most part a mistake. He deludes himself when he thinks that his wider knowledge and greater experience will enable him to do the work as well as if he had still the young man's powers of action.

Foster. Old age did not dim the artist's eye nor enfeeble the hand of Titian or Tintoretto, nor abate the military genius of Radetzky or Moltke; and Michael Angelo was between eighty and ninety when he planned and superintended the building of the dome of St. Peter's, — hanging the Pantheon in heaven, as he said.

The Squire. You carry too many guns for me. I might plead that artists are hardly men of action, or that exceptions prove the rule; but I confess that I have "generalized from too few particulars." I was thinking chiefly of our old generals in the first Afghan war and in the Crimea, and our old statesmen in the last fifty years of our parliamentary history. Gibbon says, in his stately style, of one of the Roman emperors that he put an interval between life and death. I believe he means that he abdicated and went into a convent; but, without advising the conditions of the convent, I have no doubt that he is both the wisest and the happiest old man who does abdicate the functions of a life of action, and so in fact puts an interval between life and death. Thus he may sit down, pleasantly enough, in sight of his home, and, like Souvestre's conscript, consider.

Foster. And tell us, whose service is still going on, something both interesting and instructive about his own experiences in that service.

The Squire. We will hope so. Indeed, I often think that there is a use to the world in the occurrence of this interval between life and death, if both the old and the young employ it rightly. But the old man must beware of the besetting sin of such old age.

Foster. What is that?

The Squire. Garrulous twaddle. Shakespeare, whom no form or condition of man's life escapes, has given us the picture of this garrulousness in Dogberry, Justice Shallow, and Polonius; but I need not quote him to you.

Foster. Who is, or was, Souvestre?

The Squire. Émile Souvestre was a French man of letters in what I suppose I must call the last generation, though he was only six years older than myself. The son of an officer of engineers, and educated for the bar, he had early entered on a literary career in Paris, full of promise, when the death of his elder brother and the loss of the family property threw upon him the support of his widowed mother and sister-in-law. To provide for them he at once left Paris to enter on the humble

work of serving customers behind the counter,
and doing the other retail business of a book-
seller in Nantes with whom he found employment. His literary ability and moral worth
were soon recognized by one of those customers, a deputy and a man of wealth, who was
engaged in plans for the better education of
his countrymen. Souvestre's services were engaged for the conduct of a college founded by
this gentleman ; then he became a professor
of rhetoric and editor of a newspaper at Brest,
while occupying himself with other literary
work also. Thence he eventually returned to
Paris, where he spent the rest of his life,
diversified only by visits to the provinces and
to French Switzerland for the purpose of giving
lectures to the crowded audiences which always
welcomed him. He was eminently patriotic ;
the ruling motive — I might say passion — of
his life was the education (the culture, moral
and religious, even more than the intellectual
culture) of his countrymen. We English are
apt to pride ourselves on our love of duty, but
no Englishman makes duty the guiding star of
his life more than did Souvestre. It is the
keynote of everything he writes. And what he
taught he had first tried and practiced in his
own life. "In his own heart he first kept
school ;" and those who knew him most in-
timately said that the sense of duty, which was

always strong and even stern to himself, only showed itself in perfect love to those around him.

Foster. What did he write?

The Squire. Though he died at the age of forty-eight, he left nearly seventy volumes. His history of his native and loved Brittany, "Les Derniers Bretons," is full of life and interest as well as of local and literary research, and is recognized as classical. But his chief literary work — I speak not of his lectures, but of his books — was that of story-telling. He has given us an infinite variety of tales of French life in town and country, all of which are true idyls. The characters as well as the incidents are full of dramatic interest. The high and generous moral spirit which guides their destiny is never obtruded. It is the atmosphere which we really though unconsciously breathe. And though I do not pretend to pronounce judgment on style in any language but English, I think I may call that writing terse, lucid, and graceful which was crowned with the approval of the Académie Française; but a still higher eulogy was bestowed by that learned body upon Souvestre when they granted to his widow the testimonial founded by M. Lambert in recognition of the man who had been most useful to his country.

Foster. Have any of his books been translated into English?

The Squire. His "Philosophe sous les Toits," "Confessions d'un Ouvrier," and two or three of the tales of Brittany were translated by one with whose hand my own was joined in the task; and of these the first was reprinted in America. His longer work, "Les Derniers Bretons," was, absurdly enough, translated into English from a German version, — the consequence, as the publisher said to me, of the bad habit of not reading prefaces. And another translator has published one of his longer tales with the title of "Leaves from a Family Journal."

Foster. Did you know him well?

The Squire. I feel ready to say Yes, though I never saw him. Here is his own way of answering the question in a letter to his translator. (Takes a letter from a drawer and reads.)

"Et maintenant, madame, permettez-moi d'ajouter de vifs et sincères remerciments pour l'honneur que vous avez fait à l'auteur en choisissant son livre pour être traduit dans votre langue; c'est une distinction dont il se tient fort touché. Vouloir traduire un livre, c'est prouver qu'on entre en sympathie avec celui qui l'a écrit, et qu'on sent, qu'on pense comme lui. Il n'est rien de plus doux que ces adhésions obtenues de loin, et il y a un charme

particulier dans les *amis inconnus* qui répondent
à votre cœur sans que vous avez jamais entendu
leur voix."[1]

Of such unknown friends none lives so
present to my memory as Émile Souvestre.

Foster. That must be the best kind of memory. But a memory for facts and words is a
good thing, too, and must, I suppose, be an
essential qualification for writing history.

The Squire. Gibbon's memory must have
been at once enormous and minute; Niebuhr
wrote down his quotations of chapter and
verse without needing to refer to the books
themselves; Johannes von Müller could repeat the pedigrees of all the little German
princes; and Macaulay could tell the names
in succession, and backwards as well as for-
wards, of the Archbishops of Canterbury or
the Popes, or both. A host of other instances
of verbal memory crowd on me; the prettiest,
if not the most important, is the story of Pope
reading his " Rape of the Lock " to Parnell.

[1] " And now, madam, allow me to add my most sincere
thanks for the honor you have done the author in choosing
his book for translation into your own language; it is a distinction which he feels very sensibly. To resolve to translate
a book is to give proof of hearty sympathy with the writer of
it, and of feeling and thinking like himself. Nothing is more
gratifying than to receive such assurances of sympathy from
a distance, and there is a peculiar charm in the unknown
friends whose hearts answer to your own, though you have
never heard their voices."

Foster. What is that? I do not remember it.

The Squire. Pope read the first canto of his new poem to Parnell. Parnell said, "I am sure I have heard those lines before, — I think in a monkish Latin original." Pope declared that they were all his own; but Parnell persisted, and said he would find and send them to Pope. And on his return home he sent Pope — to his great annoyance till the truth was known — the Latin verses, which I think I can repeat, as well as Pope's own. Pope's lines are : —

" And now, unveil'd, the Toilet stands display'd,
Each silver vase in mystic order laid.
First, rob'd in white, the nymph intent adores,
With head uncover'd, the cosmetic powers.
A heavenly Image in the glass appears,
To that she bends, to that her eyes she rears;
Th' inferior Priestess, at her altar's side,
Trembling, begins the sacred rites of Pride.
Unnumber'd treasures ope at once, and here
The various offerings of the world appear;
From each she nicely culls with curious toil,
And decks the Goddess with the glittering spoil.
This casket India's glowing gems unlocks,
And all Arabia breathes from yonder box.
The Tortoise here and Elephant unite,
Transformed to combs, the speckled and the white.
Here files of pins extend their shining rows,
Puffs, Powders, Patches, Bibles, Billet-doux.
Now awful beauty puts on all its arms;
The fair each moment rises in her charms,
Repairs her smiles, awakens every grace,
And calls forth all the wonders of her face;
Sees by degrees a purer blush arise,
And keener lightnings quicken in her eyes.

The busy sylphs surround their darling care;
These set the head, and those divide the hair;
Some fold the sleeve, whilst others plait the gown;
And Betty 's praised for labours not her own."

And these are Parnell's : —

" Et nunc dilectum speculum, pro more retectum,
Emicat in mensâ, quæ splendet pyxide densâ.
Tum primum lymphâ se purgat candida nympha;
Jamque sine mendâ, cœlestis imago videnda,
Nuda caput, bellos retinet, regit, implet, ocellos.
Hâc stupet explorans, seu cultûs numen adorans.
Inferior claram Pythonissa apparet ad aram,
Fertque tibi cautè dicatque superbia I lautè,
Dona venusta ; oris quæ cunctis, plena laboris,
Excerpta explorat, dominamque deamque decorat.
Pyxide devotâ, se pandit hic India tota,
Et tota ex istâ transpirat Arabia cistâ :
Testudo hic flectit dum se mea Lesbia pectit ;
Atque elephas lentè te pectit, Lesbia, dente ;
Hunc maculis nôris, nivei jacet ille coloris.
Hic jacet et mundè mundus muliebris abundè ;
Spinula resplendens æris longo ordine pendens,
Pulvis suavis odore, et epistola suavis amore.
Induit arma ergo, Veneris pulcherrima virgo,
Pulchrior in præsens tempus de tempore crescens ;
Jam reparat risus, jam surgit gratia visûs,
Jam promit cultu miracula latentia vultu ;
Pigmina jam miscet, quo plus sua purpura gliscet,
Et geminans bellis splendet magè fulgor ocellis.
Stant Lemures muti, nymphæ intentique saluti,
Hic figit zonam, capiti locat ille coronam,
Hæc manicis formam, plicis dat et altera normam ;
Et tibi vel Betty, tibi vel nitidissima Letty I
Gloria factorum temerè conceditur horum."

You see they are a very exact representation
of Pope, and monkish leonine hexameters.

Foster. Why do you call them leonine, and where is the story to be found?

The Squire. I believe they are called leonine because a lion's tail has, or was supposed to have, a tuft in the middle, and another at its end. But as to where I got the story, — I got it from my father; but whether you will find it in the books told as I have told it, I do not know.

Foster. You have always a good memory, Squire, for this kind of story.

The Squire. So my friends are kind enough to tell me. But I doubt it. I am certainly wanting in the sort of memory we were just now talking of, as possessed by Macaulay and others; and I should say that, as far as my own observation goes, the recollection of good stories, family traditions, and other memories of a like kind, are not so much recollections of the things themselves as they actually happened or were told, but rather pictures which have gradually taken shape and color in the narrator's imagination with such apparent distinctness and reality that he seems to himself and his friends to be showing them a collection of photographs, when in truth they are pictures in the composition of which there may be any amount of art combined with nature, and of fiction with fact. My brothers, old men, fond of family traditions and good stories, tell these each in a different way; and yet they are all clear headed and well informed. Sir Walter Raleigh asked how it could be possible to know rightly what happened in old times, when he found that he could not get accurate information as to something which was happening under the very window of his prison.

Foster. Then, like your Welsh or Irish judge, we must decline to hear more than one account of the matter, and write that down at once. So I hope I am well advised in keeping a journal.

The Squire.

> " A chiel 's amang you taking notes,
> And, faith, he 'll prent it."

Foster. Shall you object if I am lucky enough to find a publisher?

The Squire. No. I think we all like to see ourselves in print ; certainly I do.

Foster. I have often wished that you had a Talking Oak in your avenue.

The Squire. Or, still better, a Writing Boswell, a ghostly predecessor of yourself, my dear Foster, who might appear from time to time from behind some sliding panel with his notebook, and read out his notes of the talk that has gone on for nearly six hundred years in this old house. If he could not tell us more than we know of the dispute between the two giants about the battlemented wall, he might tell us how to fill in the meagre outline of episcopal and royal records about William de Sutton and Basilia de Sutton (his aunt or sister, as I guess), who lived in the tower in the first half of the fourteenth century.

Foster. What are those records?

The Squire. In 1315, the bishop wrote to William de Sutton entreating him "of his charity" to undertake the guardianship of the mismanaged revenues of the neighboring nunnery of Barrow; but the control was ineffectual, for, some years later, we find instructions to "restrain the prioress Joanna from wandering abroad," followed by a consistorial inquiry into the continual wasting of the revenues upon the burdensome family (*onerosa familia*) and the lodgers of the prioress, in which inquiry the sub-prioress was assisted by Basilia de Sutton, who was eventually herself made prioress after the death of Agnes, who had succeeded for a few months on the resignation of the discredited Joanna. But William de Sutton's services to the Church did not prevent his maintaining his claims against her. In the *placita*, or "Pleas" of 1322, we find him complaining before the king's judges of the trespass of the servants of the rector of the adjoining parish of Stanton Drew, and the parson's servant replying that he, the parson, had the right of pasturage after the crop had been taken off.

Foster. The old, never-ending feud of squire and parson. But how was it that the knight did not take law into his own hands, and seize the rector's cows without more ado?

The Squire. I remember suggesting this very question to Freeman here in the tower; and he said that we must not think of the mediæval knights in England as if they had the habits of those robber knights of Germany and France; for in England there were very few such men. The English mediæval knight, he said, was for the most part a man carrying on perpetual small lawsuits at Westminster about rights of land. That ghostly Boswell could tell us when the tower was built, and who added the "old Manor Place" where Leland found Sir John St. Loe; what was the talk that went on between the knight and his visitor, who so accurately observed and carefully recorded everything that he saw or heard:— then we might hear how, in the next generation, Building Bess talked over her plans for improvement and those talks between John Locke and John Strachey, to the renewal of which Locke looked forward with so much pleasure on his return from Holland.

Foster. You told me the other day who wrote the article on Nonsense in the "Quarterly," so you can tell me something about the unpublished Eclogue which is alluded to, but not given, in the article.

The Squire. Here it is. The "competitors," as the Clown in "Twelfth Night" would have called them, are Mr. and Mrs. Symonds, who were, like Lear himself, spending the winter at Cannes. You may take this copy, — I have another; and when you "prent" your notes, put this Eclogue into them. There will be no breach of confidence in doing so. (The Squire reads.)

ECLOGUE.

(Composed at Cannes, December 9, 1867.)

Edwardus. What makes you look so black, so glum, so cross?
Is it neuralgia, headache, or remorse?
Johannes. What makes you look as cross, or even more so, —
Less like a man than is a broken torso?
Edw. What if my life is odious, should I grin?
If you are savage, need I care a pin?
Joh. And if I suffer, am I then an owl?
May I not frown and grind my teeth and growl?
Edw. Of course you may; but may not I growl, too?
May I not frown and grind my teeth like you?
Joh. See Catherine comes! To her, to her,
Let each his several miseries refer:
She shall decide whose woes are least or worst,
And which, as growler, shall rank last or first.
Catherine. Proceed to growl in silence. I'll attend,
And hear your foolish growlings to the end:
And when they're done, I shall correctly judge
Which of your griefs are real or only fudge.
Begin; let each his mournful voice prepare,
(And, pray! however angry, do not swear!)
Joh. We came abroad for warmth, and find sharp cold;
Cannes is an imposition, and we're sold.

Edw. Why did I leave my native land to find
Sharp hailstones, snow, and most disgusting wind?
Joh. What boots it that we orange trees or lemon see,
If we must suffer from *such* vile inclemency?
Edw. Why did I take the lodgings I have got,
Where all I don't want is? All I want, not?
Joh. Last week I called aloud, Oh! oh! oh! oh!
The ground is wholly overspread with snow!
Is that, at any rate, a theme for mirth
Which makes a sugar-cake of all the earth?
Edw. Why must I sneeze and snuffle, groan and cough,
If my hat 's on my head, or if it 's off?
Why must I sink all poetry in this prose,
The everlasting blowing of my nose?
Joh. When I walk out, the mud my footsteps clogs;
Besides, I suffer from attacks of dogs.
Edw. Me a vast awful bulldog, black and brown,
Completely terrified when near the town;
As calves perceiving butchers, trembling, reel,
So did *my* calves the approaching monster feel.
Joh. Already from two rooms we 're driven away,
Because the beastly chimneys smoke all day:
Is this a trifle, say? Is this a joke,
That we, like hams, should be becooked in smoke?
Edw. Say! what avails it that my servant speak
Italian, English, Arabic, and Greek,
Besides Albanian? If he don't speak French,
How can he ask for salt, or shrimps, or tench?
Joh. When on the foolish hearth fresh wood I place,
It whistles, sings, and squeaks before my face;
And if it does, unless the fire burns bright,
And if it does, yet squeaks, how can I write?
Edw. Alas, I needs must go and call on swells;
And they may say, " Pray draw me the Estrelles."
On one I went last week to leave a card:
The swell was out, the servant eyed me hard.
" This chap 's a thief disguised," his face exprest.
If I go there again I may be blest!
Joh. Why must I suffer in this wind and gloom?
Roomatics in a vile cold attic room?

Edw. Swells drive about the road with haste and fury,
As Jehu drove about all over Jewry.
Just now, while walking slowly, I was all but
Run over by the Lady Emma Talbot,
Whom not long since a lovely babe I knew,
With eyes and cap-ribbons of perfect blue.

Joh. Downstairs and upstairs eve·y blessed minute
There's each room with pianofortes in it.
How can I write with noises such as those,
And being always discomposed, compose?

Edw. Seven Germans through my garden lately strayed,
And all on instruments of torture played;
They blew, they screamed, they yelled. How can I paint
Unless my room is quiet, which it ain't?

Joh. How can I study if a hundred flies
Each moment blunder into both my eyes?

Edw. How can I draw with green, or blue, or red,
If flies and beetles vex my old bald head?

Joh. How can I translate German metaphys-
Ics, if mosquitoes round my forehead whizz?

Edw. I've bought some bacon, (though it's much too fat,)
But round the house there prowls a hideous cat;
Once should I see my bacon in her mouth,
What care I if my rooms look north or south?

Joh. Pain from a pane in one cracked window comes,
Which sings and whistles, buzzes, shrieks and hums;
In vain amain with pain the pane with this chord,
I fain would strain to stop the beastly *discord*!

Edw. If rain and wind and snow and such like ills
Continue here, how shall I pay my bills?
For who through cold and slush and rain will come
To see my drawings, and to purchase some?
And if they don't, what destiny is mine?
How can I ever get to Palestine?

Joh. The blinding sun strikes through the olive-trees,
When I walk out, and always makes me sneeze.

Edw. Next door, if all night long the moon is shining
There sits a dog, who wakes me up with whining.

Cath. Forbear! you both are bores, you've growled enough!
No longer will I listen to such stuff!

All men have nuisances and bores to afflict 'um;
Hark, then, and bow to my official dictum!
For you, Johannes, there is most excuse,
(Some interruptions are the very deuce;)
You're younger than the other cove, who surely
Might have some sense; besides, you're somewhat poorly.
This, therefore, is my sentence: that you nurse
The Baby for seven hours, and nothing worse.
For you, Edwardus, I shall say no more
Than that your griefs are fudge, yourself a bore.
Return at once to cold, stewed, minced, hashed mutton,
To wristbands ever guiltless of a button,
To raging winds and sea, (where don't you wish
Your luck may ever let you catch one fish?)
To make large drawings nobody will buy,
To paint oil pictures which will never dry,
To write new books which nobody will read,
To drink weak tea, on tough old pigs to feed,
Till springtime brings the birds and leaves and flowers,
And time restores a world of happier hours.

Foster. It is very good, and certainly ought to find a place among Lear's works. It is quite a new kind among the many sorts of Nonsense, the variety of which is one of their characteristics. Did you know Lear well?

The Squire. I was not one of his early friends; but I had friends among these, and latterly I saw him often, here, or in his own house, or mine, on the Riviera. He was a warm-hearted, affectionate man, with a craving for sympathy expressed in his whole manner, and which was no doubt heightened by his having no more of home life than was afforded him by his old Albanian man-servant and his tailless cat Foss. He loved children, as his nonsense books so abundantly bear witness; and many of his songs and stories were either written for this or that child, or given to him or her, in his own handwriting and with his own inimitable pictures. One of my nieces had " The Owl and the Pussy Cat," and one of my sons " The Duck and the Kangaroo," and "Calico Pie," in what may be called the originals, — one of them in a letter signed " Yours affectionately, Derry down derry dumps; " and my daughter has a series of heraldic representations of Foss, proper, couchant, passant, rampant, regardant, dansant, a-'untin, drawn for her on the backs of letters. His letters to his grown-up friends were embellished in like manner. When he wrote to ask me to inquire about a new hotel above the Lake of Como, where he had thought of spending the summer till he heard a report that there was smallpox there, he illustrated the inquiry by a sketch of himself covered with spots ; and when writing to ask where he could hear of some friends who always traveled with a lapdog, he represented the dog overtopping the whole of the party. He sometimes, too, sent his grown-up friends some of his verses ; he sent me the then unpublished conclusion of Mr. and Mrs. Discobbolos.

Foster. I have heard that the connoisseurs

of art — critics, or whatever you call them —
see some fault in his serious pictures, but I
forget what it is. They seem to me very good,
especially those taken on the Nile. But only
a true artist could have drawn those nonsense
outlines in all their variety. Then, too, how
appropriate is the music to which he married
his immortal caricature of pen and pencil!
But is it true that much of this music has been
lost to us because he did not know how to
write down what he had composed?

The Squire. I fear it is so; though he published some of the music to which he has so
admirably set not only his own comic verses,
but several of Tennyson's songs. There is
much more that can now live only in the
memory of those who knew and loved him.
I say "loved," because he was eminently a
man of whom it might be said, —

> "And you must love him ere to you
> He will seem worthy of your love."

I recall the image of the genial old man, with
his black spectacles, or rather goggles, his
gaunt figure, and his face expressive of mingled
fun and melancholy, as he showed us his pic-
turesque house at San Remo, or, later in the
day, sat down at the piano in our room at the
hotel, and played and sang to his own music
his own pathetic nonsense of the " Yonghy
Bonghy Bò." It may seem absurd to you, as

it certainly would to many people, to say that
in that song, so overflowing with nonsense,
the old man was making fun of his deepest
thoughts and feelings, — fun because they lay
too deep for words. Villa Tennyson, so named
after his friend, was a bachelor's home of
mixed comfort and discomfort, with its garden of half-tropical flowers going down to the
shore on which the blue Mediterranean was
ever lapping, while the thick olive woods were
sloping up the hills. It is impossible not
to think of the abode "in the middle of the
woods, on the Coast of Coromandel, where
the early pumpkins blow," or to look up and
down in imagination the dusty highroad which
runs east and west, and not expect to see the
heap of stones on which the Lady Jingly Jones
might be sitting, with her milk-white hens of
Dorking. I have not the least ground for
saying that these fictions have any foundation
in fact ; but there they are, as the good old
man has given them to us.

Foster. Do you think that Lear would have
said, with Wordsworth's Matthew, —

> " If there be one who need bemoan
> His kindred laid in earth,
> The household hearts that were his own,
> It is the man of mirth " ?

The Squire. I do not know ; but the " household hearts " of old Matthew were those of

wife and child, and these Lear had not. You
are right to remember that Wordsworth is not
deploring old age generally, but the old age of
the man of mirth. Wordsworth liked paradox,
as his great "Ode on Immortality" shows ; and
those beautiful lines on Matthew are full of it.

Foster. What do you mean by paradox? Is
not what he says true?

The Squire. It seems to be becoming the
fashion to use "paradox" as a fine expression
for "false ;" but "paradox" properly means
"contrary to common opinion," and it may be
used in either the good or the bad sense. It
may be a true or a false statement, according
as the popular opinion which it contravenes is
right or wrong. In the poem you refer to,
Wordsworth, with dramatic propriety, puts into
the mouth of Matthew the paradoxical assertion that

> "the wiser mind
> Mourns less for what age takes away
> Than what it leaves behind."

Now, this is untrue as a general proposition,
though true of the particular case to which
Matthew afterwards limits it ; and the paradoxical effect is produced by his first putting
it forward as if the general proposition were
true. It is not true that the old man who can
no longer see to read regrets this less than he
does that he can still see the trees and the

sunshine and the faces of those dear to him ; for he does not regret at all, but is very glad that all these are still left to him. It is because so much is left behind that the old man is able to bear with so little regret the loss of what age takes away. But when Matthew goes on to define and limit his statement, it becomes clear and true enough. He is speaking of the " man of mirth," of the man of mirth in his old age, whose kindred are in the grave ; then, when tender but now hardly sad memories of the "household hearts that were his own" come upon him, and he can say, "The will of God be done," it jars on him to be asked to play the fool for the amusement of the thoughtless though affectionate youth who knows nothing — for he has had no experience — of these things.

Foster. You spoke of dramatic propriety. I suppose you refer to Wordsworth's own explanation that he had not given a matter-of-fact description of the active old schoolmaster of Hawkshead, but a poetical picture, in which, as in that of the Wanderer, he had introduced traits of character from other men, so as to make a dramatic whole. These are not his words, but, if I remember rightly, this is the sense of them.

The Squire. So I understand him. True poet as he is, he gives us no abstract philo-

sophical disquisition on old age in general, or
portrait of an actual old man; nor, what would
be no less undramatic and untrue to nature, a
picture of a Frankenstein in whom all characteristics of all old men are brought into an
impossible combination. Those three poems,
"Matthew," "The Two April Mornings," and
"The Fountain," make up one work of art of
a very perfect kind. It will bear any analysis
and any criticism, and come out all the brighter
and the more beautiful.

Foster. I see what you mean. The Matthew
of Wordsworth is an ideal man, and so having
the individuality, and therefore the limitations,
of any real man, and without which he would
be a mere monster, and not a man at all. He
is "a gray-haired man of glee," who even in
his old age still carries his love of fun to such
a height that it may be properly called "mad-
ness." But in all this mad fun there come
intervals of deep melancholy and sadness,
such as indeed I suppose we all have noticed
in men of wild high spirits. So much I see;
but does he not mean more than this?

The Squire. The poet brings out the rest by
the introduction of the other personage of the
drama, himself, as he was the youthful, and
therefore thoughtless though affectionate companion of the old man. In after years he
remembered, what he could not at the time

understand, that, in answer to his youthful
demand for renewed fun, old Matthew would
give way to the melancholy reflection that men
like himself

> " Are pressed by heavy laws ;
> And often, glad no more,
> We wear a face of joy, because
> We have been glad of yore."

It is not the loss of his Emma which now
makes him sad, — he can think of it, and say
from his heart, "The will of God be done ;"
but he thinks that if he had still with him "the
household hearts that were his own," he might,
like the birds, sing his merry carols, or be
silent and forgetful at his own will, and not
be bound, as he now is, to pay that heavy price
for the affection, real though it is, of his
youthful friend. What a pathos there is in the
reply of the old, childless man to the youth's
offer, at once affectionate and thoughtless, —
what should he know of death? — when he
offers himself to supply the place of the children gone !

> " Alas ! it cannot be."

Perhaps we might say that the craving, the
unsatisfied craving for sympathy, at any cost,
is the keynote, the motive, of this beautiful
little trilogy. Yet those are not the last words.
The poet, true to life and to his art, ends with
the old man, after all, singing again the witty

rhymes about the crazy clock. Soldiers strike up a merry tune as they march back from the burial of a comrade. Joy, not sorrow, is the last word.

> " The dead are not dead, but alive ! "

It was time for me to be going. We joined the ladies in the Great Parlor, and the elder lady said, " We are sorry you must go, Mr. Foster, but I hope you will keep your promise." The Squire asked, " What was that ? " And his daughter-in-law replied, " We told Mr. Foster of the custom of the Guest Book at my uncle's, in which every visitor is expected to write something, on his going away. And we proposed that he should give us some such farewell."

The Squire. Well, Foster, what did, or do, you say ?

Foster. I quoted Puffendorf and Grotius, or at least Shakespeare and Walter Scott : —

> "Stand not upon the order of your going,
> But go at once ; "

and

> "' On, Stanley, on !'
> Were the last words of Marmion ; "

and I suggested, though the lines were not very complimentary to myself, —

> " He fitted the halter and traversed the cart,
> And often took leave, yet seemed loath to depart."

But I was told that none of these were original, and so I promised to produce something of my own.

The Squire. And what is it?

Foster. I must make a confession. I had cudgeled my prosaic brains to no purpose, vainly trying to say something appropriate. Then I thought of your translation of what Sa'di had said on a like occasion; and I have made a paraphrase of that. (Takes a paper from his pocket and reads.)

> Through France and Germany I 've wandered,
> And sometimes laughed, and sometimes pondered
> How men in country and in city
> Were rude or friendly, dull or witty.
> I 've lived in Naples and in Rome,
> But nothing like this English home
> In all my travels did I find,
> No place so fair, no folk so kind,
> Nor of such genial heart and mind.
> And now my holiday is done,
> And I, unwilling, must be gone.
> I still would keep the memory green
> Of all that I have heard and seen:
> The Giant's battlemented wall,
> The portraits hanging in the Hall,
> The Terrace and the Waterfall,
> The Lanes, the Oaks, the old knight's Tower,
> My lady's Parlor and her Bower;
> The welcome of the eldest Son,
> When he the Election fought and won;
> The pleasant talk we had together,
> " What news to-day?" or " How 's the weather?"
> Then changing to a loftier strain,
> 'T would rise and fall, and rise again,

And tell of all I loved to hear :
Of Shakespeare, Milton, Maurice, Lear ;
Of Persian Poets ; how men read
The language of the Arrowhead ;
Of Love and Marriage, Life and Death ;
Of worlds above, around, beneath.
Nor, Ladies, is the day forgot
When we rode down to Camelot,
And Arthur, Launcelot, and Elaine
Seemed in that hour to live again.
And though I take a careless leave,
Nor wear my heart upon my sleeve,
These memories never will decay
Nor fade into the light of common day.

The Squire. Bravo, Foster! Your version of Sa'di reminds me of Sir John Cutmore's silk stockings, which were mended with worsted till there was not a thread of the old silk left.

Foster. I do not pretend to compare myself with Sa'di ; but if I had five minutes to spare, I should like to appeal to the judgment of the ladies, as to the silk stockings, by reading your translation of the Persian lines.[1]

Then came the English good-by, which says so little and means so much ; and as I left the room I heard the Squire say, half to himself, " And, faith, he 'll prent it."

I crossed the north court, and as I passed through the gateway in the wall I looked back, and saw the Squire, with his children and grandchildren, standing at the door under the tower.

[1] See Appendix.

APPENDIX.

INTRODUCTION TO THE BŪSTĀN OF SHAIKH MUSHLIHU-D-DÍN SA'DI SHÍRÁZÍ.

I desire to acknowledge that, though not unfamiliar with the original, I have, from lack of eyesight or a Persian reader, availed myself in making this translation of the more literal version and the notes of Colonel H. Wilberforce, Clarke, R. E.

IN THE NAME OF GOD, THE MERCIFUL, THE COMPASSIONATE!

In the Lord's name! Who did all life create!
The Wise! Who taught man speech articulate!
The Lord, the Giver, the Help in time of need!
The Merciful! Who hears when sinners plead!
The Great! From Him who so shall turn away,
Greatness shall seek in vain, seek where he may;
Kings, who lift up their heads in pride of place,
Bowed down before His throne themselves abase.
He is not quick to judge the unruly heart,
Nor pleading culprits sternly bid depart.
The Sea of Knowledge, infinite, divine,
Doth in each drop two elements combine:
Justice and Mercy, — neither of these can fail;
He sees the sin, and, pitying, draws the veil.
Though evil deeds bring down the wrath of Heaven,
He who turns back, repentant, is forgiven.
Against a father should a son rebel,
Unmeasured wrath the father's breast will swell:
Displeased, the kinsman owns his kin no more,
And drives him like a stranger from his door:

If to thy friend thou shouldst unfriendly be,
He breaks the fellowship and flies from thee:
The servant slothful in his daily tasks
Promotion of his master vainly asks:
And if the soldier in his duty fail,
No plea will with his king and chief avail:—
But He, Lord of the noble and the base,
Against no rebel shuts the door of grace.
The fair Earth is his table, duly spread;
He asks not, "Friend or foe?" Welcomed are all, and
      fed.
If he were quick to mark iniquity,
Who from His anger could in safety be?
His nature knows no change: His kingdom stands
Needing no help from man's or angel's hands.
All things, all persons, serve His kingly state;
Man, beast, fowl, ant, and fly, upon Him wait.
For them His Bounteous table He prepares;
Which even the lonely, far off Simurgh [1] shares.
That bounteous love in all His works He shows;
He grasps the world, and all its secrets knows.
His Will is law, His greatness all things own,
Whose kingdom is of old, with rivals none.
On one man's head He sets a monarch's crown,
One from a throne He to the dust brings down.
From Him the cap of fortune *this* receives,
To *that* the beggar's garb of rags He gives.
If He should bid unsheath the avenging sword,
The Cherubim, silent, obey His word:
Should He proclaim the fulness of His grace,
The Lost One cries, "I, too, have there a place."
Before the greatness of His royal state,
The great ones of the earth their pride abate;

---

[1] The Phoenix or Griffin of Oriental legend dwells at the
end of the world.

To those who are distressed, in mercy near,
And ready still the suppliant's prayer to hear.
Things yet to be are present to His eye,
Secrets untold before Him open lie.
All heights and depths confess his guardian hand;
Before his judgment seat all peoples stand:
None but bow down before Him and obey;
None on His work a censuring finger lay.
Planned in His mind unborn creation stood,
He called it forth, and saw that it was good.
From East to West the Sun and Moon He sent
And o'er the waters spread the firmament.
The world with earthquake reel'd till on its edge
He firmly fixed each mountain like a wedge.
The sons of men in angel's form He made,
But must not paintings on the water fade?
He sets the rose upon the branch of green,
Ruby and turquoise hides in rock unseen.
Should seed on land, raindrop on ocean fall,[1]
This makes the pearl, and *that* the cypress tall.
No atom can to Him remain unknown
To Whom the seen and the unseen are one.
For snake and ant He daily food prepares,
Although nor hands nor feet nor strength are theirs.
All things to be He in His mind portrayed;
Of things that are not, things that are, He made:
Then bade all things to nothingness return
Yet there to wait the resurrection morn.
His Godhead is eternal, all confess:
His substance and His essence none can guess.
His Majesty and Power are infinite:
No eye can take them in, no words recite.
The bird, Imagination, soars in vain,

1 The Eastern poets held that the pearl was a drop of rain
which had fallen into an open oyster, and there been trans-
muted.

The hilltops of His being to attain :
Reason, upon a sea of storm-tost waves
Embarked, those whirling waters vainly braves :
A thousand ships have in that sea gone down,
And not one plank upon the shore is thrown.
Whole nights I sat, lost to the world around,
As were my spirit on some journey bound :
When a strange terror took me by surprise,
And plucked me by the sleeve, and said, " Arise."
God, by His knowledge, rules His kingdom well :
The mazes of His Nature none can tell.
His substance hidden deep from human eye,
His attributes, by thought unfathomed, lie.
To Souhbar's [1] eloquence we may attain,
To know God's nature we shall search in vain.
Rash man upon this quest may urge his horse,
But words of warning [2] check his eager course :
It is not always well to ride at speed ;
'T is sometimes better to hold in your steed.
And should the traveller find that hidden way,
The door of his return is shut for aye.
Who of the chalice at that banquet drink,
Entranced, their senses in oblivion sink.
That hawk has seeled eyes to Heaven unturned,
This with eyes open, and with feathers burned. [8]
None on the treasure of Karoon [4] has come,
Or, finding it, has found the road back home.
He who that journey and that search would make,
Thought of return forever must forsake.
Perfumes of Love Divine around thee play,

[1] An Arab poet.
[2] *La ahsa.* " His praises are more than can be numbered."
I suppose the words are from the Koran.
[3] That is, by the fire of divine love.
[4] A hero of the family of Moses and Aaron in Arabian
legend, supposed to possess great treasures.

He asks, "Am I thy God?"[1] Thou answ'rest, "Yea."
Seek out with earnest search the things above;
Thence to God's Presence rise on wings of love.
By Truth the veils of earth and sense are riven,
And Glory is the only veil of Heaven.[2]
Seek'st thou by earthly roads to find thy way?
Surprise will seize thy rein and bid thee stay.
Only man's Guardian has crossed o'er that sea,
And those whom he has bidden — " Follow me."
He who has journeyed on, without this Friend,
Worn-out, has failed to reach his journey's end.
Oh, Sa'di, think not man has ever gone
Along the Path of Holiness alone,
But only he who treads behind the Chosen One.

IN PRAISE OF THE PROPHET: TO HIM BE PEACE.

Generous of disposition! Full of grace!
Prophet and Intercessor of our race!
Chief of the Prophets! Leader of the road!
Faithful to God! Where Gabriel found abode![8]
The Guide! The Intercessor! Lord of all
Gathered for judgment at the last Great Call!

[1] It is related of the preëxisting souls of the descendants of Adam, that were to be, that each was asked by the Creator, "Am I thy God?" Each soul that answered "Yes" was born to be a follower of Muhammed, while those that were silent were born to be infidels.

[2] The sara-pardah — the curtain drawn before the throne of the Eastern king, to hide him from the public gaze. So the veil before the Mercy seat in the Jewish Temple was the symbol of the invisible king. And the words of Sa'di, " there remained no Sara Pardah but glory," correspond exactly to those of St. Paul: " Dwelling in the light which no man can approach unto."

[8] Faithfully recording in the Koran the revelations brought down by Gabriel from God.

Speaker from out the heavenly Sinai's height!
All other lights but borrowed from that light!
His one Book, while it yet unfinished lay,
Purged libraries of other faiths away:
When he in wrath the sword of terror drew
By miracle he cleft the Moon in two!
His fame, when through the world its course it took,
The Courts of Kings as with an earthquake shook!
"THERE IS NO GOD BUT GOD:"—Lo! at that
        sound
The idols Lat and 'Uzza bit the ground.[1]
Those idols' dust he scattered to the wind
While ever the truer faiths he left behind.
One night he sat, in vision rapt, and through
The Heavens he passed, as towards God's throne he
        drew,
And through the angel hosts he passed his way
In majesty and grandeur more than they:
He onward passed the nearer road to find
While even Gabriel remained behind.
"Mount boldly higher" (the Prophet thus began),
"Thou Bearer of the Word of God to Man:
When thou didst me sincere in friendship prove,
Why didst thou thus draw in the reins of love?"
Gabriel replied, "No power to mount have I;
Higher my wings are powerless to fly:
Should I one hair's breadth higher attempt a flight
I burn my wings in that effulgent light."
None for his sins in prison need remain
Who can, for guide, a lord like thee obtain.
To thee what praise acceptable can be!
O Prophet of our race, peace be on thee!
May angels' benedictions on thee rest,

---

[1] Lat or Alliat and Al 'Uzza were two of the three idol god-
desses of the Arabians which were destroyed by Muhammed.

And with thee be thy friends and followers blest !
O happy Guide, no loss of dignity
Falls on thee in the Court of the Most High,
When some poor humble uninvited guest
Goes in with thee to share the heavenly feast.
God's praise and honor rested on thy head
While Gabriel kissed the ground where thou didst tread.
The Heavens bow down before a higher than they,
Not made, like man, of water and mere clay.
First of create existence thou ; from thee
All else existent only offshoots be.
What can I say to thee ! No words of mine
Can speak the praises that are rightly thine :
It matters not : the Book, in heaven-sent words
To all thy greatness honor due accords.[1]
What more can Sa'di, humble poet, say ?
O Prophet, blessings be on thee alway !

THE REASON FOR COMPOSING THE BOOK.

Through many far-off lands I, wondering, went;
With men of every kind my days I spent :
To me each corner did some pleasure yield,
I gleaned some ears from every harvest field.
So pure of heart, and of such humble mind,
None like the men of Shiraz did I find :
Blest be that land ! It won my heart away
From cities famous for Imperial sway.
'T was pain to leave a garden all so fair,
And not some token to my friends to bear.
Methought, when travellers from Egypt come,
They bring back sweetmeats to their friends at home :
And if no sweetmeats in my hand I bring,
Words sweeter far than sugar poets sing.

---

[1] Alluding to the words in the Koran, " But for thee, O Mahammed, I had not created the sky."

Those sugared sweetmeats men but seem to eat,
In books the wise store up the real sweet.
A palace of Instruction then I framed,
And set therein ten gates, which thus I named : —
First, Justice, Counsel, Order, How kings should reign,
And in the fear of God their rule maintain :
The next Beneficence, by which we can
Praise God in dealing forth His gifts to Man.
The third, Love : — not of passion and of sense
In man, but Love of God, deep and intense.
The fourth, Humility : Resignation next.
The sixth, Contentment, by no troubles vexed.
The seventh, Education ; how to rule
And train yourself, and in your heart keep school.
The eighth, Thanksgiving for the Almighty's care :
The ninth, Repentance ; and the tenth gate, Prayer.
In an auspicious day, and happy hour,
And in the year six hundred fifty-four,[1]
My Book I finished, filled this treasury
With store of pearls, of truth and poetry.
But still I fear my jewels to display ;
And on my hands my head in doubt I lay !
For oyster shells and pearls are in one sea,
One garden holds the scrub-bush and the tree,
Yet have I heard, O man of generous mind,
The generous critic loves not fault to find ;
The silken robe with gay embroidery shines,
Yet that silk robe a cotton quilting lines.
Then if the cotton in my verse you see,
Be not severe, but hide it generously.
I boast not of my costly wares, but stand
And humbly ask for alms with out-held hand.
I have heard that in the day of hope and fear,

---

[1] But that "rhymes the rudders are of verses," this date
should be 655 A. H., answering to 1250 A. D.

That day when all before the Judge appear,
He will, in mercy, bid them all to live,
And for the righteous' sake the bad forgive.
Thou, too, if badness in my verse shouldst see,
Do thou likewise: be merciful to me.
When in a thousand one good verse you find
Withhold your censure, be humane and kind.
Of such a work as mine 't is true, indeed,
That Persia land of letters has no need:
Far off with awe you hear me, like a drum,
But find the music rough when near I come.
You say, What brings this Sa'di, bold-faced man?
Roses to rose beds, pepper to Hindustan?
So, too, the date with sugar-encrusted skin: —
You strip it back, and find a bone within.

THE PRAISE OF ABŪ BAKR.[1]

I was no courtier, born and prompt to sing
With courtier's tongue the praises of a king:
But in the coming times might question be
Of one who threaded pearls of poesy;
When Sa'di bore the palm of verse away
Who then was King? "Abū-Bakr," we might say.
No unfit boast — the Prophet even would tell
That in the Just King's days his own birth fell.[2]
Oh, Guardian of the faith, the law, the throne,
No name since Omar's has like thine been known!
Chief of the chief ones, crown'd among the crown'd,
And still for justice through the world renown'd;
He who seeks shelter from life's stormy blast
Here, and here only, shelter finds at last;

[1] The reigning Atâbak. The Atâbaks named by the poet
were in succession from father to son, Zangi, Sa'd, Abū Bakr,
Muhammed Sa'd.

[2] Naushirwan. Muhammed says, "I was born in the time
of the Just King."

Welcome that door to all who fly from wrong
As men by each broad road to Mecca throng.
In no land else so rich a heritage
I see for prince and people, youth and age.
No sorrower to this prince his grief imparts,
But finds with him a balm for suffering hearts.
About his crown the skies their splendor shed,
While on the ground he humbly bows his head.
'T is natural that the poor should sue and wait:
But humbleness shows goodness in the great;
The common man the common road has trod,
The humble ruler is a man of God.
The monarch's liberal doings now may hide,
The sound thereof though all the world spreads wide.
So wise a man, so worthy of his lot,
The world, since world it was, remembers not.
In this thy day no sorrower grieves for wrong
Wrought by the Oppressor's grasp unjust and strong.
Such Government, such customs, and such law
Not ev'n Firidun [1] in his glory saw.
Great is his honor in the Almighty's sight,
That he upholds the weak ones by his might.
Over the world his shadow so is spread
That lawless force awakes in age no dread.
Men bear with groans, in every age and clime,
The changes and the violence of the time.
Oh, mighty monarch, under thy just reign
Of wrongs of time and fortune none complain.
Thy people dwell in peace; but after thee,
I know not what that people's end will be.
But happy thine own fortune, on that morn
When Sa'di in thy land and day was born.
So long the sun and moon still climb the sky,
The memory of thy name shall live for aye.

---

[1] Firidun was said to have reigned in Persia in 750 B. C.

If former kings a name for good have won,
They learned the way to walk from sire to son:
But Thou, by thine own rule, dost far outshine
The gathered glories of a royal line.
Alexander built a wall of stone and brass
The hordes of Gog and Magog might not pass:[1]
When o'er the world the hordes of Changis roll'd
The wall that saved thy kingdom was of gold.
The poet who, in thy just rule secure,
Sings not thy praises, let him sing no more.
Oh, sea of bounty, of all gifts the mine,
We seek for aid and find our life in thine.
I cannot count the virtues of the king,
Nor can within this book their record bring,
If Sa'di would thy virtues tell aright,
Truly another book he must indite.
But cease from thanks for all thy generous care:
'T is better that I spread the hand of prayer!
The world be at thy feet, and Heaven thy friend!
The world's Creator keep thee and defend!
Thy star, ascendant, lights up all the skies,
And with its fire burns up thine enemies.
Let not the revolutions of the age
Bring grief to thee, on thee pour out its rage:
A single sorrow in the heart of kings
To a whole world a world-wide sorrow brings.
Tranquil and prosperous be thy heart and land,
Blest be the kingdom guided by thine hand.
Like thy true faith, sound may thy body be!
Weak, like his own false creed, thine enemy!

---

[1] The Eastern legends of Alexander tell that he built a
wall of brass and stone to keep out Gog and Magog, that is,
the Scythians. The later hordes of Changis (or Changes)
Khan, resembling the earlier ones in their devastations and
probably of the same race, were bought off by Abū-Bakr.

May God's strength fill with joy thine inward parts,
And in thy faith make glad thy people's hearts!
May'st thou with the Creator mercy find.
Should I say more 't were empty talk and wind.
It is enough that the Almighty one
Doth still increase the welfare of thy throne.
Sa'd did not quit the world with pain, when he
Begat a son to be renowned like thee.
That such a noble branch as this should spring
From the pure stock of Sa'd, count no strange thing;
For though his body to the dust be given,
His soul triumphant dwells in highest Heaven.
O God, send showers of grace and mercy down,
And make the memory green of Sa'd's renown!
With guiding hand fulfil his grandson's claim,
To share Sa'd's honor as he shares his name.

IN PRAISE OF MUHAMMED SA'D, SON OF ABŪ-BAKR

Son of Abū-Bakr! heir to crown and throne!
Muhammed Sa'd! good fortune all thine own.
Fresh in thy fortunes, wise among thy peers:
Old in deliberation, young in years!
Lofty in spirit, and in wisdom great,
Strong in thine arm, with hope thine heart elate.
Happy the mother of the time to be,
To cherish at her breast a son like thee!
No river floods of bounty pours like thine;
Thou risest, and the Pleiads cease to shine.
The eye of fortune beams upon thy face
Chief among Monarchs in thy pride of place.
The oyster holds the pearls, yet know we well
The pearl 's the pearl, the oyster but the shell:
Thou art that hidden pearl of price we see,
The jewel of the royal house in thee.
O God, preserve him by Thy grace from high!
Keep him from injury and the evil eye!

O God, through every land increase his fame;
And make all men love him who loves Thy Name.
Now and hereafter grant his heart's desire,
To dwell in justice, and to Heaven aspire!
Make the devices of his foes to fail;
Nor revolutions of the world prevail!
The Tree of Life still bears new fruit thereon;
The son still seeks the fame his sire has won.
All who speak evil of this House, beware,
Full evilly they and all their house shall fare.
Hail, Faith and Knowledge! Law and Justice, Hail!
Hail, Land and Throne, may that rule never fail!

www.ingramcontent.com/pod-product-compliance
Lightning Source LLC
Chambersburg PA
CBHW030356270326
41926CB00009B/1139